"A gripping memoir of desperate, go-for-broke passion and purpose."

Called to All

How I Discovered the Power of a Yielded Life

Billy Bray

WESTBOW
PRESS®
A DIVISION OF THOMAS NELSON
& ZONDERVAN

Copyright © 2017 Billy Bray.

All rights reserved. No part of this book may be used or reproduced by any means, graphic, electronic, or mechanical, including photocopying, recording, taping or by any information storage retrieval system without the written permission of the author except in the case of brief quotations embodied in critical articles and reviews.

Unless otherwise indicated, all scriptures quotations are from the Holy Bible, English Standard Version (ESV) © 2001 by Crossway Bibles, a publishing ministry of Good News Publishers. Used by permission. All rights reserved.

Scripture taken from the King James Version of the Bible.

This book is a work of non-fiction. Unless otherwise noted, the author and the publisher make no explicit guarantees as to the accuracy of the information contained in this book and in some cases, names of people and places have been altered to protect their privacy.

All italics or bolded quotations of scripture have been added by the author.

Your purchase of this book helps the next generation fulfill their call to serve. Christian Information Service, Incorporated (CIS, INC) is a not-for-profit media ministry that exists solely to serve the growth needs of next-generation mission leaders, missions and church-based projects fulfilling the vision of Matthew 24:14. Billy Bray shares a portion of every royalty received from the sale of this book with Christian missions. Your purchase helps CIS grant support to approved projects led by emerging and potential leaders. For information about these charities or the Yielded Life League, contact CIS Legacy Books, PO Box 6511, Charlottesville, VA 22906. The author personally welcomes comments and questions at bray.william@gmail.com.

WestBow Press books may be ordered through booksellers or by contacting:

WestBow Press
A Division of Thomas Nelson & Zondervan
1663 Liberty Drive
Bloomington, IN 47403
www.westbowpress.com
1 (866) 928-1240

Because of the dynamic nature of the Internet, any web addresses or links contained in this book may have changed since publication and may no longer be valid. The views expressed in this work are solely those of the author and do not necessarily reflect the views of the publisher, and the publisher hereby disclaims any responsibility for them.

Any people depicted in stock imagery provided by Thinkstock are models, and such images are being used for illustrative purposes only. Certain stock imagery © Thinkstock.

ISBN: 978-1-5127-7049-0 (Softcover)
ISBN: 978-1-5127-7050-6 (Hardcover)
ISBN: 978-1-5127-7048-3 (eBook)

Library of Congress Control Number: 2016921641

Print information available on the last page.

WestBow Press rev. date: 2/13/2017

Presented To

_____

By

_____

Date

_____

On the Occasion of

_____

Share the Message of this Book.
Here's how ...

If this book becomes a valuable part of your life and calling, don't let the message die. Share the secrets of presence, purpose, and power by presenting this special gift edition to others.

Keep a supply of gift editions handy on your bookshelf. Be ready to personally inscribe and present a copy as God places someone on your heart. It is especially suitable for high school and college students, graduating seniors, overseas visitors and international students, those in military service, newlyweds, prisoners, the sick, or anyone else at a turning point in life.

Quantity discounts are available for books used in campus outreach ministries, counseling, clubs, conferences, mentoring, seminars, and libraries. To order additional gift copies at quantity discounts, contact:

Yielded Life League
Attn: Quantity Discounts
Post Office Box 6511
Charlottesville, VA 22906
www.OSMissions.org

The Yielded Life League is a not-for-profit ministry of
Overseas Students Mission and CIS
Legacy Books. It depends totally
on the contributions of Christian friends, groups and prayer circles.
All gifts are tax-deductible.

Called?

This book is for those who
know they are called,
think they might be called,
wish they were called,
seek to be called,
fear they are called, or
glad they have not been called!
In other words, it's for
all who are serious about where they are
on their spiritual journey.
It's about discovering your real purpose
and the joyful power of a yielded life.

Author Billy Bray, seen here in his early
twenties as a young missionary
refugee from the Rajasthan Blitz campaign in India

Dedications

To the next generation of yielded ones.

To the brave and kind who welcome them to alien shores.

To faithful mentors who stoke the flames of their passion for God's will to be done on earth as it is heaven.

To friends who encouraged me to write this book with prayer and finance, nagging me to share this story that has been fifty years in the making. Without you, it would not have happened.

Most of all, to my wife, who sacrificed with me every step of the way. Thank you, Ivy Sanchez Bray, my faithful companion in Christ and fellow servant of the Lord.

Acknowledgments

The author gratefully acknowledges the Rev. Earl Burton for his review of scripture application in this work, and the many friends who contributed to the manuscript as a labor of love, including my most trusted sources, David Burder and Ray Eicher. Special thanks to all the professional staff at the WestBow Press Division of Thomas Nelson/Zondervan publishers.

Contents

Dedications ix
Acknowledgments xi
Introduction: No Ordinary Book xv
Chapter 1: The Night God Talked Back 1
Chapter 2: Early Yearnings to Yield 29
Chapter 3: Choices on the Calvary Road 48
Chapter 4: A Love Supreme 62
Chapter 5: Blitz Rajasthan 1966 74
Chapter 6: When "Plan A" Fails 101
Chapter 7: Five Waypoints to a Yielded Life 126
   Saying Yes to God 127
   Knowing His Will Always 130
   Choosing to Believe It 133
   Uniting with His Body 135
   Yielding to His Spirit 138
Epilogue 145
Bibliography 151

Introduction: No Ordinary Book

For many are called but few are chosen.
—Jesus Christ (Matthew 20:16)

This is no ordinary book. It's written to be a movement, not a product—a battle cry for those hungry and longing to serve. Especially among the next generation.

Are you one? Has he called? Is he calling? Are you a chosen vessel? Could he be doing in you what he has done in me? Are you deluded or is it real?

How will you know? Will it come in an angelic visitation ... a dream ... an image ... a transcendental experience ... the written word ... a message ... a revelation ... a sense of divine presence? Will reason rule your decision?

Christ Jesus said, "Many are called but few are chosen." Are you one of them—his chosen? Shouldn't you be sure? I dare you to find out, to read and engage this message to the very end.

Could you be among us? Follow the five spiritual waypoints in my testimony and find out. You can share this love supreme, a supernatural love from above. You can find the pearl of great price.

Be sure of your heart; hungry as it is for his presence, purpose, and power. He demands purity of purpose. "Keep your heart with all vigilance for from it flow the springs of life" (Proverbs 4:23).

Start as early as possible in life, but remember that the call isn't limited to youth. Age, beauty, breeding, ethnicity, gender, nationality, or skill set does not determine your election. He who calls has his own reasons and seasons.

This book is not based merely on my experience. It is based on authentic, Word of God demands. And God cannot lie—his promises are ultimate truth. When followed, they will overcome the "killer barriers" holding you back from submission.

So, if you think there is even a remote possibility that God is calling—consider the path that unfolds in these pages. I'm not saying my story is precisely normative for you. Your details will vary, but the road map is roughly the same. There is no skipping a waypoint. Your shining path will rise to meet you as you step out and follow, one stage at a time.

If this were a self-help book, it could be titled, "101 Ways to Live the Yielded Life" or "Discipleship for Dummies." But that's not how it works. The Almighty uses process, not formula; grace, not law. There are no shortcuts.

You're unlikely to find these five waypoints featured in titles on the checkout line of your local supermarket. Those looking for instant spirituality will not find it here.

This is not about self-assertion but winning by losing. It frees you from the prison of self-effort. It helps you find God's personal, unique plan for you.

Hopefully, by the time you've finished this book, you'll never look at your "five fingers" the same. The way to find your call is right at your fingertips.

Every good read involves making a covenant with the author. So, make one with me now. Let's believe together for three things on our journey:

First, let's be practical. This "called life" is one that you can live. Millions have trod it successfully before you. These principles are eternal and universal. They work equally well in every context—you'll be able to apply them whether you end up on stage or in the audience ... running a business or presiding over government ... single or married ... in war or peace ... teaching or studying ... as doctor, nurse, or patient. They work equally well in Africa, Asia, China, Europe, India, the Middle East, or Oceana.

Second, let's be urgent and brief. From my life experiences, you'll learn to: (1) enter his presence through dialogue, hearing his voice in prayer; (2) discern his will in the Word; (3) access his power through believing faith; (4) unite in love with others, (5) yield to supernatural power. These principles last a lifetime, through every phase and stage of your earthly journey. Whether you are six or 106.

You can live in victory. You can connect to God's will. If you seek, you will find. That's not my promise. He who calls you fulfills and provides.

Third, let's handle your spiritual emergencies. Perhaps you are facing a personal spiritual crisis today. Maybe you are at a fork in the road.

Then I have good news. You can start enjoying the benefits of yielded living today. Presence, purpose and power are yours for the asking now.

Once you yield, you can begin immediately. In real time, I learned the five waypoints in less than 41 months. However, the critical decisions which took only minutes to choose have taken a lifetime to process!

In 1964, I following a voice that called me from Chicago's gold coast to the howling wasteland of Thar – the Great Indian Desert. That Spirit led me to Kota Junction (a place I had never heard of) in Rajasthan – a state on the Pakistan border!

As I obeyed, I learned to yield. I found peace with my creator, even in times of outward failure, fear, rejection and uncertainty.

This is the life I still enjoy today. It is a life I have lived on battlefields and in torture chambers, in natural and man-made disasters, in executive suites, in news rooms, broadcasting studios and at the University. This is a way of life I have lived through successes and failures, betrayals, broken hearts, misguided love affairs, marriage, divorce, parenting, and the AIDS death of a wayward child.

Through it all, I have learned that a yielded life is the only path to answer the call ... the only path to having passionate, purposeful meaning. If you choose to enjoy this kind of life, then please share our secret with your family and friends.

That's why the publishers have included a presentation page in the front of the *Legacy Gift Edition*. May you use it to pass along what you find here – a fulfilled, joyous, passionate, and yielded life.

Billy Bray, Author
Charlottesville, Virginia

Chapter 1

The Night God Talked Back

"And when they had brought their boats to land, they left everything and followed him" (Luke 5:11).

MY Christian friends and family were shocked – absolutely scandalized – when I announced my decision. It was over 50 years ago, but I can still see some of their angry, hurt and puzzled faces. Many people believed in me, admired me, and had such high hopes for my life.

"How could you go so overboard?" they asked.

Was I really going to throw my life away because of some mystical experience? Had I actually been in "The Presence" or was this a youthful delusion or hormonal attack? Had I been dreaming? Was God so unreasonable? Illogical? Demanding?

For some, my faith and radical obedience was an arrogant judgement on their lifestyles. They were very upset. Such is often the case when one says "yes" to a call from the Lord. It can provoke anger, hurt, opposition, resistance and even retribution.

We were living, after all, in a world that looked like a page out of the *Mad Men* television series. America was never richer. More affluent. Chicago was a boom town economy. Why turn your back on the blessings of God?

Hadn't I heard that the days of empire were over? India was free and independent. It was neo-colonial to hear a call to India! Is this American imperialism? The indigenous churches are on their own now. It's time for them to sink or swim.

And my inner-city, street-smart Chicago-swagger didn't help one bit. In the culture where I grew up, that was a key to survival – but it didn't come off well at Moody Bible Institute. It looked like adolescent pride, and some of it was just that. I was 16 going on 26 – city-born and bred, and it looked like I was acting like a punk.

Why in the world would God call Billy Bray anyway?

In a Bible college filled with suburbanites and farm kids, I was a second-year student, an urbane native. Living on Chicago's very hip near north side. The red lights of nearby Rush Street held no secrets from me. I loved the Gold Coast and felt at home in the Playboy lifestyle.

It was the fall of 1964 – for Chicago in general, and my social circles it was a golden age of freedom, hubris, optimism, and prosperity. I was steeped in it.

Yet at the same time, I was born in a pious home. I was full of genuine faith, seeking to serve the Lord. I was the son of a much-admired, saintly minister who was born in the Appalachian coal fields but rose to inner-city leadership. My dad, Chaplain Al Bray, was known all over the greater Chicagoland area.

It was cool to be an evangelical then. Billy Graham was on the cover of Time Magazine. His crusades made it into Life Magazine and onto Network TV – the Internet of the day.

We evangelicals had just arrived on the media scene; back then we were a fast-growing, vibrant, powerful voice for God in the community. These were the days when Billy Graham still advised the pope and the presidents.

In this world, we had achieved a certain respect; my family had clout and status in a corrupt, Catholic city. That meant a lot to all the important people in our circles.

Now, I had upset all that by obeying a call to foreign missions.

Hearing such a bizarre call from on high was scary and threatening. Family, fiancé, peers and teachers were all stunned. This was the kind of thing that only happened in story books. Maybe to Francis of Assisi, Poor Clare or St. "Mother Theresa" of Kolkata – but not to a bright, young preacher boy who had everything going for him in the "real world" of the Windy City.

Even mission-minded friends, who should have cheered the news, didn't. They too were puzzled. Does God really call someone so young, so radically, so soon, and so absolutely?

That mythic, historical Christian figures might get such a call was one thing – that Billy Bray would get it was quite another! Billy was not a Nate Saint or Elizabeth Elliot. Most of my friends doubted that that the same God who called William Carey, Dwight Moody, Hudson Taylor, St. Ignatius or St. Patrick, was still in the business of missions – or that he was calling Chaplain Bray's oldest boy into His service in India.

Born after midnight – When God talked back to me

So how did this journey of discovery begin? It happened during a half night of prayer. It was the turning point for me. Mystical. Miraculous. Supernatural. It was born after midnight early in the new semester, probably about September 1964.

However, don't jump to conclusions. I am not saying that my kind of mystical experience is normative or prescriptive for you. I did not seek it that night; would not seek it again today. Nor would I urge others to seek such phenomena.

I am not saying that God will show you his will exactly as he showed it to me, but I do know that you will find him when "you search for him with all your heart" (Jeremiah 29:13-14). And the Lord will give you the direction you need in your life—most probably from the written word.

However, he knows you far better than you know yourself and will give you the assurance you need in just the way you need it.

Maybe God will speak to you miraculously, as he did to me. He still does. He still might. Jesus is Lord. He can and does send angels ... visions ... dreams ... but he is just as likely to appear in what the Bible calls a "still small voice."

In this case, I sought God quite innocently and without design. I was not looking for signs or wonders. However, I cried out to God. I wanted him more than anything else. I entered his presence. I deliberately sought him.

I said yes to God, and he talked back to me in the only way I would have understood at that point in my life.

Heaven Takes Our Cries Seriously

Heaven took my cry seriously, and the Lord gave me what I needed to shake me out of spiritual blindness. The bottom-line lesson is clear: be very, very mindful when you dare to make inquiries, promises, vows, or pledges to the Lord. God takes your words seriously.

It began about curfew time, around 10:30 p.m. when the women students melted demurely out of a second-floor prayer room in Fitzwater Hall. I was left alone, bent over in my chair, staring at the huge India map spread at my feet—one of those giant ones from the Geographical Survey of India (GSI).

As the only male that year in the India Prayer Band at MBI, I was quite out of place. In fact, I was more "lured" into this circle of "seeking women" than elected president.

(It all began with an innocent schoolboy crush on my charming and shapely mission's professor, a vivacious former missionary to India who sponsored the group. Unable to say no to her nomination, I let myself be chosen—all even though I had only passing interest in India.)

Now alone with the map, I had a rush of guilt. I knew my more pious sisters were still praying. They planned to reassemble in the Houten Hall girls' dorm to carry on without me. There, I knew, they would fervently be pleading with heaven for the souls of Hindus and Muslims in South Asia.

And more than one would be praying for me as I alone waited on God in Fitzwater, the towering building topped by the WMBI Radio tower and the Moody Radio Network.

As they left, I remained on my knees, too ashamed to say or do what was really in my heart. I was on my honor to stay and pray, and my honor was running thin at that moment.

I Was a Spiritual Poser—Playing a Game with God

You see, I was a spiritual poser. My thoughts were no longer on prayer! I was a secret media junkie, and this was my chance to check the news before turning in for the night. No one, I reasoned, would ever know that I wasn't spending the next ninety minutes in prayer.

However, these Missionary Prayer Band meetings were mandatory at Moody then, a leftover discipline from the Victorian era.

For me, they were just "not working." I was going through the motions of intercession like a zombie—pretending to do something I really didn't understand. I wasn't praying in "faith-believing." I was not expecting to see God's hand actually move. I wasn't united with the others in the circle.

I never shed a tear for the lost.

In fact, I wasn't really seeking his presence; I didn't have a clue to what spiritual warfare was all about! This was merely another religious exercise to me, a legalistic formula that I did because it was expected. I was praying in a way that Jesus had condemned—to be seen of others.

I was in fact a modern-day Pharisee, a religious hypocrite.

I viewed prayer mostly as part of the marketing mix for a special event or public relations campaign. It helped with the offerings. It was part of the total religious experience around something like the Billy Graham Evangelistic Crusade, an event I had recently "worked" every night at McCormick Place on Lake Michigan.

Not that I didn't pray selfishly every day for my own wants and wishes! I had a daily quiet time, but even then, God was still kind of a cosmic Santa Claus to me. I mostly sat on his knee going over my list of demands and wishes, seeking his blessings on my ambitions, dreams, and hopes.

The fact was this: the only thing I really prayed fervently about was my own personal career, love life, and good grades on the next test. I wasn't praying to God as much as praying to myself—but the Lord was merciful to me anyway.

Up till that midnight hour, I viewed group prayer as an emotional, feminine response to a lost world. It was okay for women, but what was really needed, I felt, was more love in action (primarily led by me, the man of action, always cast prominently in the spotlight).

In fact, I was proud to be a religious and social activist, and prayer just wasn't an "action" in my mind. Waiting on God made no sense to me. In other words, what I really preferred was a short prayer of blessing before my work began. I got along very well with the memorized table grace before a meal!

Even at mealtimes, before the "amen" had barely been pronounced, I would butt in with my next remark.

But That Night Was Different ...

Then something happened. A burst of shame overtook me. I began to think of the women praying on without me. Of their sincere prayers for India, Pakistan, and all the nations they had never seen. If they could watch and pray into the night, then so could I.

After all, I scolded myself, I was president of India Prayer Band, and it was my duty to stay up and pray through. Every student had to join a prayer band back then, but few of us (myself included) sought the face of God. Most were like me, just going through the motions. Prayer was part of our religious ritual.

It was, I reasoned, a historically important part of every great revival and missionary movement. I had heard talks about the First and Second Great Awakenings in America. About the Haystack Prayer Meeting at Williams College, the Student Volunteer Movement—the National Collegiate Day of Prayer. But I had never seen this. I had not yet been in a revival.

Duty Takes Over, and I Seek His Face

So, I decided I would pray because it was the right thing to do. I owed it to the women to keep praying. I would pray in solidarity even if I didn't feel like it, even if I didn't understand their passion.

They believed in prayer, after all. What kind of hypocrite would let them think I was praying into the night with them when I was focused on media instead?

I changed. I repented. I began to offer a prayer of sacrifice in total trust without my usual hypocrisy. I prayed according to Psalm 5, "Lead me, O Lord, in your righteousness .... make your way straight before me."

Then God answered with his presence. The atmosphere changed. I was praying alone to him, not for the watching crowd. Perhaps for the first time, I was in that "secret prayer closet" described in Matthew 6:6.

"But when you pray, go into your room and shut the door and pray to your Father who is in secret. And your Father who sees in secret will reward you openly."

Looking back, I think that was my first baby step in discovering the yielded life, the first and earliest waypoint on my journey to the throne of God.

I began to draw near to God, as James commanded, and God started to draw near to me. That night, for one of the first times in my life, I was in a dialogue with God. I sought, and I found. I knocked, and the door opened. I asked, and I received.

After a few minutes, I did something new and unusual for me. I was getting drowsy. I realized if I just sat or kneeled there, I would soon fall asleep on my knees. So, copying something I had seen George do the summer before in Europe, I crawled onto that big wall map of South Asia.

There I was on all fours.

This was not cool. George had seemed like such an embarrassing fool to me back in Forest Hill, England—praying on a map that way, on the floor. Who was he kidding? I was way too sophisticated for that. Now, it made perfect sense to me. I was in private with God.

Somehow as I knelt on that map, India exploded into reality before me. It became so real that I almost felt I was there.

It was an old political field map, probably printed on canvas during the British Raj. It had incredibly detailed drawings showing airfields, railway junctions and terminals, rivers, districts, ports, states, and territories.

"Lord Jesus," I vowed out loud, "I'm going to pray to the Father in your name for every state in India before I go to bed."

Maybe that simple vow, made in the name that is so painful to the devil spirits of India, aroused the darkness. At any rate, I was no longer alone in the room. Although I didn't yet know it, other evil forces had joined the prayer meeting!

You see, the spirit world is not as far away as we think. It is right there next to us in another dimension. I felt as if I had just been attacked by what Jesus describes in Matthew 16:18 as "the gates of hell."

Suddenly, the demon birds of the air were gathering around me. The seed had fallen into my heart, and they were determined to snatch it away before it could take root and grow. As Christ explained in the parable of the sower and the soils, there is a real devil determined to steal away the Word of God from our hearts.

Still determined to stay awake, I began walking around the edges of the map. Sometimes falling back onto my hands and knees, I started to pray my way from the Himalayan Kingdom of Nepal to the isles of Sri Lanka (Ceylon on that old map). Mysteriously, my soul continued to melt into the geography from Myanmar (Burma) to Afghanistan.

Just as the demon powers were about to take me out with sleep, I prayed out loud, singing faith choruses to better concentrate. Soon a spiritual power from on high came over me, and I had added energy not my own. Then it happened.

Spiritual Warfare Breaks out around Me

Suddenly, a cosmic, spiritual struggle erupted. I felt both the angels and demons present. An angelic messenger of the Lord was helping me wrestle with those "spiritual forces of wickedness in heavenly places" described in Ephesians 6:12.

"For we do not wrestle against flesh and blood, but against the rulers, against the authorities, against the cosmic powers over this present darkness, against the spiritual forces of evil in the heavenly places."

I was in the spiritual battle for places I'd never heard of until that night. I lost all track of time and began to pray for many cities and towns in Rajasthan whose names I couldn't even pronounce: Ajmer, Alwar, Bikaner, Jaisalmer, Jaipur, Jodhpur, and Udaipur.

This was very different from any previous prayer I had ever experienced. This time I was not mouthing empty words into the air. Something else happened. God spoke back. The Holy

Spirit of God was in the room with me. I was uttering blessings and curses. I was speaking into existence things that were not.

The Lord had my full attention, and then I sensed a magnetic power pulling me toward that one state on the map.

From out of the howling wastes of Thar, the Great Indian Desert, an angry force reached out to me. The enormous weight of this spiritual creature seemed to paralyze me as I prayed for Rajasthan. I couldn't take my hands off the state.

In the west and center was that vast dessert surrounded by a ring road that seemed to end and begin at a place called Kota Junction. The state had a long, long border with Pakistan and Punjab.

New Delhi, the capital, seemed to sit atop Rajasthan like a crown. I didn't know it then, but I was touching the spiritual heart of India, territory Satan was determined never to yield.

I flattened out on the map. Unable to move. Overwhelmed by that gravitas and presence that goes about like a roaring lion. I knew that I was weaker than this one who wanted to devour me, but I also knew I was not alone. The Lord God Almighty and His angel host are much stronger than our foe.

I Was Terrified—Was I Getting a Call?

Until that night, I had never even heard of Rajasthan or Kota Junction or Jaipur or Maru-Kantar—the Desert Thar. Why was God making such a big deal out of this place on the map?

I feared "the worst."

Was this "a call" to India? Could it be that the Almighty One was somehow planning to send me to go to Rajasthan? To India? Even though I was president of India Prayer Band, I still had no interest in going anywhere near India. The last place on earth I wanted to visit was India. I pictured it as dirty, dusty, hopeless, and starving—scenes of famine in Bihar were my concept of India.

A Land of Blood and Terror

But something compelled me to pray on. I didn't know that I was in prayer for some of the bloodiest real estate on earth—a place of jihad crusades by Muslim conquerors against Hindus and Sikh defenders. Terrorism was a way of life.

The Rajput's who ruled the land were so strong that when the British invaded, even they wisely sued for peace. Some of the Rajas stayed independent throughout the history of British India.

Nor did I know that it was a place of incredible injustice and violence against Dalits, women, and children, a place of human bondage and slavery that was still resisting the light of Jesus Christ and his body.

I also didn't know that this was a heartland of Arya Semaj, a Hindu version of the Muslim Taliban. It was a spin-off from this fanatical movement in Poona that helped assonate the Hindu father of modern India, Mahatma Gandhi.

Out of this crazed hate group came the birth of a bloody era of terrorism that grew in Afghanistan, Pakistan, and Punjab—throughout North India—killing one million souls during Partition in 1947 and three million more during the Liberation of Bangladesh.

And the bloodshed goes on and on. As I write, there are almost daily terrorist attacks in this belt of violence and religious extremism. As I wrote this, on an Easter Sunday, over sixty-five Christian women and children were killed by an ISIS bomber in Lahore. The demons continue to torment their Hindu and Muslim captives with violence that often spills over to harm the Christian community as well.

These same devil spirits are the demons behind the ISIS jihad and the Islamic State terrorists. The spirit of partition didn't stop when India and Pakistan split. In fact, it continues around the world today through conflicts in Europe, Nigeria, Northern Iraq, Syria, and the United States. I didn't understand all this at the time, of course.

What I did know that night was that God was alive and talking to me. He was calling me to pray for this area known by demographers as the Saffron Crescent. And Satan was fuming mad that I had touched his masterpiece of hatred and idolatry.

Now I know that was happening. Like the way in which Jesus was tempted after the Father baptized him with Holy Spirit, I was being tempted and terrorized by demon spirits. Satan's hosts reached out halfway around the world to resist my prayers in Chicago. Time and space means nothing in the spirit world. My pure, innocent faith was an existential threat to their hold on India and Pakistan—and the battle is global.

In prayer, I felt the power of the Holy Spirit within me, binding and losing the savage spirits that Satan has assigned to keep India in his bloody grip. And I knew that the victory was the Lord's.

No Negotiating with These Forces

This was an amazing moment of revelation for me. Up until this time, my spiritual experiences had been mostly cerebral and intellectual. God and the spirit world he rules were not just invisible but unimaginable to me.

Somehow, up until that moment in my life, I felt that I had God on a leash—and the devil too. In my mind, I was keeping God in a box or cage, and I could take him out when I needed him (which was almost never). In my everyday behavior, I was like the wicked man in Psalm 36:1 who had "no fear of God before his eyes." But all that was about to change.

Instantly as I lay there helpless, I knew there was no negotiating with the forces I had encountered in this hour of prayer. I felt like any resistance on my part would be met by an unstoppable force. Unless I took up the full armor of God, it was obvious that I could never hope to "stand firm against the schemes of the devil." I had to obey Ephesians 6:11:

"Put on the whole armor of God, that you may be able to stand against the schemes of the devil."

Moody Bible Institute, like much of the North Shore, was built on landfill and swampland. As I resisted Satan in prayer, I had a vision. I was resisting a hideous force seeking to press me through the floor and into the clays of the Lake Michigan just below us.

It was as if the demons were crying out to me as well.

"Look," they taunted, "you cannot take Rajasthan from us. This is our territory, and the people want us here. We're not giving up our deserts to you."

I cried out to God, "What are you saying to me, Lord? Do you want me to go to Rajasthan? Surely there are other places where my skills can be better used?"

Only silence from God. Yet I knew he was present. I was not standing against the forces of hell alone. He was present with his angels as my defense and shield.

My only college sport was wrestling. I was on the Moody wrestling squad, so I knew what it was to be pinned to a mat. Now, God or my spiritual opponents—I couldn't tell which—had me pinned me to spot halfway around the world I had never heard of—a place called Rajasthan.

I was troubled by the implications of all this. I couldn't really explain it, so I decided not to try. Like Mary, the virgin mother of Jesus, I decided to keep this revelation in my heart. I pondered it often but only shared it with a handful. It seemed weird and mysterious to me ... miraculous ... impossible ... ridiculous. God could not be calling me to India or Rajasthan.

Yet, I had just had a transcendental experience. God and the devil were both profoundly real to me. India beckoned.

So, I summited as Mary did when she was visited by Angel Gabriel, "behold, I am the servant of the Lord; let it be to me according to your word" (Luke 1:38). I too was willing to yield, although I didn't understand. If that meant India (and I hoped it didn't), then so be it.

Triumph of Miss Turner and Her "Vestal Virgins for India"

All this was totally out of character with my natural inclinations. This tentative yielding to a call was still a most reluctant one. There was none of the usual "Hey look at me" drama and showmanship I usually employed.

India was his initiative, not mine. God had set me up for this "date with destiny" through the prayers and witness of three people. Besides my first mentors, Lew Williams and George, God used an older sister, Rosemary Turner.

Miss Turner was my first-year missions' professor at MBI. Though at least twenty years my senior, she was a sparkling "old maid" by zestful choice. I had never met a woman who so deliberately choose to throw over marriage for the sake of Christ.

Joyfully, she had the supernatural grace to ignore this personal sacrifice for Jesus with unconscious humor and zeal. At first, I pitied her. Like my roommate, Lew, her love for God was so great that she didn't view her sacrifices as sacrifices.

Rosemary was my first prayer partner and our resident "Elizabeth Elliot" at Moody. In an atmosphere that carefully cultivated and exalted domestic ambitions for the women students, she modeled a life devoted to the Lord, not diapers. (Moody trained women to various avocations and skill sets, but the first goal was to train all its young women to be helpmeets to future male clergy.)

Not Rosemary.

She was never a Betty Friedan feminist yet joyfully pursued her calling as an academic who put Christ's will above marriage and everything else. She had a devoted following among some of the women students—and a grudging admiration among the men. She was our Lottie Moon.

Her women, and she had quite a following, were the Christian equivalent of Moody's vestal virgins in my eyes.

They were sold out. They loved the Lord. Like those with Nazarite vows, they had devoted themselves to him.

They were putting Christ ahead of marriage, something that in the 1950s and sixties was unthinkable to women of a certain age. Most of the girls at Moody were there to get a husband, and there was no shame in that—but not this group.

Rosemary challenged and led them. Dressed always in tightly fitted saris and stylish Punjabis, she was never a wallflower. A former TEAM missionary, she loved life—and was a model of chastity and self-sacrifice.

Most especially she loved all things Indian and Pakistani—food, fashion, language, and music. That is what it takes to be cross-cultural, to have a burden for a people not your own. She was an ambassador for Christ and for India, a charming guide to one of the world's greatest and largest cultures.

She made India fun and attractive. She loved Bollywood before Bollywood was cool.

Rosemary Turner and her posse were my best fans at Moody, and without them I would never have had the human support I needed to answer the call. To my knowledge, none of them made it to India—but they were the united force that sent me. Without their support, I doubt I would have obeyed the Lord.

God can and does use everyone who yields to him. Miss Turner, just by obeying the Lord and being her academic self, was used by God to make an incredible impact on me. It came just at the point when I needed it most. Teachers, take note.

All men need feminine approval, and I needed it more than most. God knew that. So, the Holy Spirit put Miss Turner and her all-girl prayer band in my way just when I needed them most. They were my cheerleaders, my fan base, and without them, I cannot imagine how I would have ever obeyed the Lord in the days that followed. Wives, girlfriends, and mothers, take note.

Rosemary and George, the Prophets of My Calling

Fans, friends, and mentors are important. Without Rosemary Turner and George, I would never have fulfilled my "call to all"—my personal obedience to the Great Commission for India.

That eventually morphed into a realization that I really had a call to Kota Junction and North India. There can be no "sent ones" without senders; no missions without local churches and the larger Body of Christ ... but Rosemary, her women, and George were the first ones to see it—even before I did.

I didn't know it, but the Spirit of God was calling me into a large, already spiritually united, global movement. He was leading George and the Send the Light teams to India backed by a worldwide network of prayer. Oblivious to each other, we were all praying separately but in united faith-believing for Rajasthan (and all of India).

There were many Operation Esther prayer circles out there, praying in duets and trios for the nations, and I was connected spiritually to them.

At the same time, when I thought I was praying alone that night in Fitzwater Hall, there were people praying in Coimbatore, Delhi, Paris, Istanbul, and Sydney!

George was fascinated by India because it was one of the final spiritual frontiers on earth—and still is today. It had more unreached people groups (URGs) than any other country (over 3000). It was almost the exact center of what became known as the 10/40 Window, the last big territory to be reached before Christ returns.

To tell the truth, India was dimly glowing on my radar too. I had already brushed off a challenge to go there during the summer of '64 OM Blitz in Europe. After "A Summer That Counts" in Spain with Lew Williams and the Catalan team, we debriefed in England.

There, we squirmed under George's fanatical call to all; to take a break year right then and there—to stay on for the year program.

Or you could sign up for the two-year program. The call was simple, "be a foot soldier of the cross." Come and organize future blitzes into Afghanistan, India, Iraq, Iran, Lebanon, and Turkey—and other places vaguely described as "the Communist world" and "the Muslim world" and "MENA" (short for Middle East North Africa).

We were mesmerized by mass evangelism. The blitz was working in Europe. It would surely work everywhere else. In this, George and the OM leadership were thinking as most Americans do.

It was during our half nights and nights of prayer in Europe and London that I had first heard of the unmet needs and open doors, and I managed to sleep on my knees through most of them.

Places like North India or Syria, for George and other STL/OM leadership like Gordon Magnuson, were the only legitimate targets. South India and Israel were already evangelized—only resistant places like North India were still unreached.

All this "vision casting" talk I stubbornly resisted—and no place more than North India. But who knows? Thank God for those who continued to share the vision while I resisted. How much of the seed they planted was later watered by the Spirit?

My Heart Begins to Change Toward India and the Nations

So, the prayers of Rosemary and her "ladies in waiting" were being melded with others around the world. Waypoint 3 was taking place in the spiritual realm. The Lord was answering their prayers a little more each day. I amazed myself as I recognized a new "love supreme" growing in my heart. It couldn't be coming from my natural man. I had little interest in anything related to North Africa, South Asia, or the Middle East.

While my heart was changing, so did my brain. Up until then, in my head the ancient lands of China and India were inhabited mostly by gentile, heathen nations, the sons of Ishmael and daughters of Cain.

I thought these were people and places under a curse for rejecting the Messiah and the kingdom of God. I considered them to be lands and kingdoms that had missed their chance to enjoy God's favor.

Thank God, the Lord didn't share my prejudice!

I didn't accept or understand that Christ also died for the nations living in these lands. He loved them and loves them still. The mystery of the gospel is that Christ is delaying his return in order that a people will be called out for his name from these lands.

This is the reason the church is still left here on planet Earth. Christ wants us to bring in a harvest of souls from these lands; that's why he has historically blessed lands that bless missions—and weakened lands and cultures that do not. That's also why he blesses free lands where the gospel is freely preached.

How else can anyone explain the Mayflower Compact? The first American colonists formed a government of low for the glory of God and for sharing the gospel to all nations!

How else can one explain the mystery of how God used a group of British slave holders like Jefferson, Madison, and Washington during the American "Great Awakenings" to reach the nations with the gospel?

Jefferson, using the little light he had, brought religious freedom to America—and out of that came the United States and missions as I knew them, including Jefferson's efforts to reach the Indians and free African slaves.

In fact, Jefferson planted the seeds of the American Civil War that would end slavery in the United States and cause 600,000 Americans to die in order to free the slaves.

I didn't know then what I know now, that God sent Christ to die for nations as well as individuals. This has been his will all along, throughout the ages. Even ancient Israel shared this mandate. All nations were to be blessed through Abraham.

Jesus had this passion for tribes, tongues, and nations, "And this Gospel of the Kingdom will be proclaimed throughout all the whole world as a testimony to all nations, and then the end will come" (Matthew 24:14). God is withholding his inevitable judgment on anti-Christ kings and kingdoms until we reach all nations.

All this learning and revelation was taking place in my heart before the days of the Internet of course. All my research about Rajasthan was library based. As I searched through encyclopedias and back issues of the *National Geographic*, I found that Rajasthan was a place of camels, beautiful women in colorful saris, and rifle-toting warriors. It was a place of courageous, hard-working people groups.

For centuries, it had resisted the Assyrians, Persians, Greeks, Romans, Moguls, numerous jihads, and finally the British colonizers. Throughout history, most human empires ended their maps at the Hindu Kush for good reason!

I was struck by how intensely rural it was, very agricultural.

"That place couldn't be for me," I said to myself confidently. "I'm nobody when it comes to reaching farmers or suffering masses for Jesus. I can't learn languages or work with Muslims or Hindus. I'm not a social worker or a doctor.

"God wouldn't send me there. He must have a better place for me, somewhere on a news desk in the USA or Europe."

True Discipleship, Radically Forsaking All to Follow Him

Something else was going on in my life. The Lord was dealing with my general resistance to his will as well as my particular resistance to India.

Soon after that half night of prayer for India, I began to be personally radicalized by my reading of the gospel, especially Christ's demands in Matthew and most especially in the gospel of Luke. Those hard questions and demands that Jesus made of the first disciples were getting through to me.

It was like I had never seen these commands and requirements before.

In the gospel of Luke, the words of Lord Jesus burned off the pages and into my soul—and my will was bending to his in those important adolescent choices regarding my future family, fortune, and vocation.

This I believe was the second of my third baby steps toward the yielded life. American culture, the spirit of this world, had lost its grip on me. I was slowly breaking free. The Holy Spirit was weaning me away from my idols.

What Does It Really Mean to Love the World?

I was raised in a world of often-superficial religious legalism, a culture where dancing, drinking, movies, and pop music were considered worldly—but now for the first time, I was beginning to see that my "worldliness" was much more than that.

We evangelicals were still in love with the world—standards and values created by Madison Avenue, the media and education...and I was one of them, now seeking to be free. I was in love with Jesus. I wanted to follow him all the way now.

Among my critics and peers, no one could believe that I was really taking Christ's commands seriously. Those far more sophisticated countered Christ's commands with well-honed arguments and theology.

They had a lot of biblical, dispensational, and ecclesiastical logic carefully structured to show that the Lord couldn't really mean what he said in Matthew and Luke about the costs of following him.

Most of all, they agreed emphatically, he could not actually be calling me to leave home and family to obey the so-called great commission commands. Serving God, they insisted, didn't demand my deliberately choosing sacrifice, suffering, or hardship.

"Jesus," they argued, "could not possibly mean what he said to his disciples in the gospels. You are taking the Bible too literally."

- He couldn't really mean Luke 14:33, "So therefore, no one of you can be my disciple who does not give up all his own possessions," as it says in the New American Standard Version of the Bible or "... any one of you who does not renounce all that he has cannot be my disciple," as it says in the ESV.
- He couldn't really mean Matthew 10:38–39, "And whoever does not take his cross and follow me is not worthy of me. Whoever finds his life will lose it, and whoever loses his life for my sake will find it."
- He couldn't mean, "And a person's enemies will be those of his own household. Whoever loves father or mother more than me is not worthy of me, and whoever loves son or daughter more than me is not worthy of me" (Matthew 10:36–37).
- He couldn't really mean Luke 14:26, "If anyone comes to me and does not hate his own father and mother and wife and children and brothers and sisters, yes and even his own life, he cannot be my disciple."

About this time, I met William McDonald, president at the Emmaus Bible School in Oak Park, Illinois. He was the author of a little booklet called *True Discipleship*. It was a book something akin to what David Platt's book *Radical* is today.

Like George, Lew, and others on the STL/OM team, he was taking up his cross and following Jesus. He left behind security, money, convenience, family, and career for the Lord. He was strong, sensible, and level-headed. He was an authentic, distinguished leader and definitely not crazy. I couldn't think of any reason I shouldn't follow him.

My parents chose to live lives of poverty to reach inner-city Chicago and the poor. They were a living model of this kind of life. Why shouldn't I follow their examples?

The more I studied these so called "hard sayings of Christ," the more sense they made. The efforts to soften his stark demands only confirmed their absolute meanings. For example, they said "hate" meant "love less" in Luke 14:26. While that softened the hyperbole a little, it still meant the same thing. *Nothing, even family relationships, is to come before our loyalty to Christ.*

The same is true for Matthew 10:38–39. "Take up your cross," the professors said, should be translated, "take on the will of another." If I granted that, it didn't change the ultimate meaning, "whoever loses his life for my sake will find it."

I was willing and ready to lose my life for him. The clincher was my roommate, Lew Williams. While I struggled with these scripture texts, I was living with a guy who was living them out before my very eyes.

Lew had only one change of clothes. My wardrobe filled the closet and spilled over into suitcases under my bed. Lew ate just enough to live "while I lived to eat"—often going back for seconds and thirds of sweets I didn't need. Lew, on the other hand, didn't buy what he didn't need—he wasn't collecting things. He sold everything he didn't need but always had plenty of books and tapes to give away.

And it wasn't just in material things. Lew was living out the spirit-controlled life before my very eyes. He was praying about everything, deliberately loving others as he loved himself. I learned more from Lew's silent example than from anything he ever said or preached.

Preparations for Monterrey Mexico Christmas Campaign 1964

Other apostolic actions radicalized me for Christ's life of love during this time. My appointment from George as STL/OM leader on the Moody campus in '64–65 made me a *teacher* of the yielded life—and short-term missions made me a *practitioner*. In those two years, I did four short-term missions: Canada, Mexico, South Side Chicago, and Spain.

These were the days before cassette tapes, CDs, and today's audio file downloads. So, we played reel-to-reel training tapes from George on basic subjects such as the role of scripture in our lives, love, faith-believing prayer, discipleship, mentoring faithful men, spirit-filled living, and submission in team and church life, unity, and apostolic action.

Most life transforming for me was the absolute commands of Christ to take the gospel to all nations in Matthew 24:14, 28:28, Mark 16:15, Luke 24:49, John 3. His promises of power to do so in Acts 1:8, Mark 16, and Matthew 28.

Then, there was John 14:6, "Jesus said to him, "I am the way, and the truth, and the life. No one comes to the Father except through me." I'll never forget George's pleadings regarding Christ's absolute claims. If what he said in that verse was true, then we had to go. We could allow nothing in our lives that might immobilize us.

The words of Christ became so real to me that I was absolutely without excuse. I could and I would go in simple obedience. As the winter break mission to Mexico grew closer, I started selling what I didn't need, living with only a couple changes of clothes and giving my savings to the mission.

People noticed.

The more I literally obeyed the Word of God, the more arguments I heard against going. Thankfully not everyone opposed my decision. I began to build up a team of prayer partners that stood behind me, including my home church pastor—but most of my clergy friends, family, peers, students, and teachers began to undermine my plans and zeal for the Lord's work.

The Time Was Right—God Had Opened the Doors

Slowly I accepted the idea God was calling me right into missions without delay. The time was right. The Middle East was at peace and relatively free for the first time in centuries. Most Muslims despised radical Islam then—and there was virtually no Muslim Brotherhood, ISIS or al-Qaeda. Both the Shah of Iran and the House of Said were friendly to the United States. George insisted that the doors to India and the Middle East were either open or opening to Americans. Globalization seemed attractive, and fanatical nationalism was in decline.

Plus, Christ was calling me in the Word. I decided I would go and take as many with me as I could. During our Christmas campaign in Monterrey, Mexico, I decided that I would go public with my decision when I got home.

I had heard the call, and it was the right time and place to announce bold, sacrificial decisions—decisions that I had not really thought through yet. This was Moody Bible Institute, the "West Point of Christian Service."

But even at Moody in the early 1960s no one was expected to just announce that he or she was going to quit school at the end of the year and go to the mission's field!

People Were Really Concerned about Me ...

People were instantly concerned and worried about me. Was Billy Bray going too far with this mission thing? Most *but not all* my peers thought I was crazy. Some of my professors believed I had just temporarily gone off the deep end. My deans recommended counseling. My fiancée and her family was terrorized. My family was in shock.

Most were sure I had just gone off on an emotional whim and would "get over it" once they talked some sense into me. And talk they did, both to my face and behind my back. I was soon the object of adoration, pity, or scorn.

You see, a bright young leader with a great future didn't quit school and go overseas to sell books door-to-door and pass out literature in the streets. Maybe for a summer on a short-term mission but not on a one-way ticket with no plans or way to come home.

This broke the mold. I was signing up with Send the Light, a.k.a. Operation Mobilization. It was a literature mission group then widely mocked for being "gypsies for Jesus." Many accused George of being an extremist cult leader who seduced his followers into selling everything and moving overseas to beg in the streets and churches as they "handed out tracts."

I Was Going "Off the Reservation"

In fact, as my critics were quick to remind me, I didn't even know where I was going. Where would it be? To Hindu India or maybe the Muslim Middle East or the Communist world? I was going off the reservation—thinking outside the box of organized religion.

"This is extremism," they began to chant in unison.

You didn't put the mission ahead of a mission board. American missions were very formalized back then—planned, safe, and insured. You joined a reputable mission board, were carefully screened and vetted, raised support, and discerned your call to a specific "mission field." This took years. Little or no risks were allowed. On the other hand, Billy Bray had no spiritual covering. No safety net. No back-up plan.

Most of all, in our circles, you didn't put missional living ahead of career planning or seminary. To do so cost me all the little academic respect I had! Ministers had to have primarily an ecclesiastical and theological education. I quickly discovered that a call and the Bible wasn't enough in this world. I was in the pastor's course at MBI on a secure, fast track to a comfortable and safe suburban pastorate.

I was the first in our family with plans to go onto college and seminary. Not to pursue higher education especially broke my father's heart. Academically and intellectually, I was the sharpest knife in the family drawer. Everyone considered me not just smart—but exceptional. That I would waste my potential on missions didn't make sense to our whole extended family.

Dad dreamed I would take over the Light Bearer's citywide chaplaincy program he led in Chicago and "take the family franchise" national. Education was key. Institutional chaplaincy was changing, growing more professional. It required at least a master's degree or equivalent.

He was head Protestant chaplain at Cook County Hospital for twenty-nine years. He served on boards of other Light Bearer's programs at twenty-eight other public institutions in California, Illinois, Indiana, and Michigan.

You didn't pass up a chance to take over your father's ministry. My dad was grooming me to become his assistant at the Light Bearers Association, and the national director of our family's mission. He was sure I would tire of serving a suburban parish. He was praying for me to do home missions, not foreign missions. I was the apple of his eye, and he was terribly disappointed at my lack of judgment.

To realize that I was willing to go wherever God might call me simply broke both their hearts, dashed their hopes that I would at least stay in Chicago. They wanted me to do what they never could because of their blue-collar backgrounds and lack of formal education.

Missions or Marriage?

In the early sixties, you didn't put missions ahead of marriage either. The American dream was not taking a young wife overseas—or for engaged couples to separate for two years at a time, serving on different continents. This decision cost me my fiancée. It broke not only her heart but the hearts of her mother and dad, my mother, and both our extended families.

In short, I was letting everyone down in my family and our religious world, becoming a fool for Christ—throwing it all away. Most of all, I was giving up the American dream as it had been defined in the 1950s following WWII.

I didn't understand what I was doing or why my choices were creating such havoc, but they were. In our denominations and churches, we had respectable ways and means of fitting Christ into our families and careers—and Christ was calling me to color outside the lines.

So, one by one, I went ahead and broke all the rules:

- I announced that I was dropping out of school,
- giving up my career plans for a life in journalism,
- abandoning my teacher's plans for seminary and the pastorate,
- surrendering my inheritance,
- walking away from my family's hopes and dreams,
- breaking off plans for marriage to my high school sweetheart.

By the time of our Summer That Counts mission to the inner city ended in 1965, I was already homeless and penniless for the cause of Christ. I had become what was then known as a "Jesus freak."

I had been accepted for the two-year Send the Light Training Program with Operation Mobilization and was scheduled to leave for Europe "and points beyond."

Freedom Means Having Nothing Left to Lose

"Freedom means having nothing left to lose," wrote Kris Kristofferson in his sixties folk hit "Me and Bobbie McGee." (Vocalist Janis Joplin went on to record this as a pop single before her death in 1971. It was released postmortem, her biggest hit ever.)

And that song of the sixties says it all. We were free and ready to go wherever the Lord sent us. We had nothing left to lose. Steve, our book team, and I could suddenly go "where needed most," and that summer it was on Chicago's South Side.

We went door-to-door in Englewood as well as the urban housing projects like Robert Taylor Homes—reaching out to Africa Americans before we went on to the nations overseas. We even went to Hyde Park; soon-to-be President Obama's old neighborhood close the University of Chicago.

The city was filled with racial tension in the summer of '65—and we were on the edge of the Age of Aquarius. We heard a strange call and made a wild choice. We had forsaken all to follow Him, throwing all into the cause of Christ.

Most of our baby-boomer peers were making similar choices that year. They were on the streets too, chanting, "Freedom now!" and, "Drugs ... sex ... rock and roll." They were portrayed as cool; we as crazy.

For the first time, I began to feel that some people just hated me without a cause. For them, just being a Christian was a reason enough. They hated us because they hated him.

What we didn't expect, was rejection from the Christian, religious community. We were learning the truth of Christ's warnings in John 16:2-3, "They will put you out of the synagogues. Indeed, the hour is coming when whoever kills you will think he is offering service to God. And they will do these things because they have not known the Father, nor me."

Obeying a call on your life has many rewards. But it can also be a costly decision in some ways; it will surely cost you everything this world offers.

Chapter 2

Early Yearnings to Yield

From infancy, you have known the Holy Scriptures that are able to give you the wisdom you need for salvation ...
—2 Timothy 3:15

From the howling wastes of Thar, the Great India Desert, a challenge had come to me—a call from the Creator and a defiant scream of resistance from the dark princes that held captive their Indian slaves. For some reason, that night in Crowell Hall, I was being spiritually prepared to go overseas on a divine appointment.

I was given just the right grace to wait upon the Lord that night—and my heart was ready to respond to his call. I was prepped by God and ready to yield.

This was not my doing. That grace was—and always is—a gift of God. And to be honest, God had been preparing me for years. Nothing happens in a vacuum.

Yet that night, in a special way, I was like the weaned child in Psalm 131. It would be wrong for me to make it appear like I came to that place of grace and surrender of my own accord. I had many spiritual models in my life, people who I watched as they waited upon the Lord.

Long before I first began to submit to the power of a yielded life, I was already bending that way.

As a Child, I Knew the Scriptures

My mother orchestrated my life from the beginning, surrounding me with the Bible. I was taught to hear and memorize the scriptures by my father. Both were missionaries, called to the nations in the inner city of Chicago.

Like Timothy, my mother raised me in the Word of God. "From infancy, you have known the Holy Scriptures that are able to give you the wisdom you need for salvation …" (2 Timothy 3:15).

I was also protected and blessed by the Lord with a host of Christ-centered role models, carefully chosen by my mother. Many people guided and prayed for me, including my aunts, babysitters, extended family, parents, pastors, scoutmasters, Sunday school teachers, and youth leaders. God-fearing people invested in my life. The Lord works in our relationships.

I actually spent sixteen years in the spiritual womb before I finally made that big push out—born after midnight on that fall night of prayer in '64. It came only after a series of smaller surrenders. Like many, I yielded one piece of my will at a time.

Tenderness toward the divine can begin much earlier than most people think. We underestimate children and teens, to dismiss their spiritual sensitivity and volition is a huge mistake. Every one of us needs to be trained from the earliest age to protect the generation behind us. Older siblings need to teach younger ones.

My backstory with Jesus began when I was still a preschooler; that's when I started making right choices in my life—long before I spent that night wrestling with spiritual powers on a map of India. And at every step of the way, I was helped by others who were yielding to God for my sake.

Called to All

Three baby steps, three choices, led me to that night in Crowell Hall:

I was only four when I made this, my first right choice.

I remember clearly when I made that first little move toward the yielded life. My vacationing family was crossing New Found Gap in the Appalachian Mountains of North Carolina and Tennessee. A huge storm crashed around our 1949 Chevy sedan.

Sheets of rain and lightning surrounded the car like ocean waves. We had just seen the "trail of tears" death march acted out in in the play *Unto These Hills* at the Cherokee Indian reservations in western North Carolina.

That tragic portrayal made a huge impact on my little mind. I could not get to sleep that night. Nightmares haunted me. Ghosts, injustice, and terror filled my little mind. Death for the first time became reality to me.

That spirit of death and danger was still impacting my mind as we climbed through the rain at New Found Gap.

"I'm going to die!" I wailed in terror during the storm. That confession ignited sympathetic wails from my baby brothers.

"I'm going to die! We're all going to die," I repeated as my seatmates joined in the shrieking chorus.

"Do something," my dad implored with a sidewise glance at my mom.

In a flurry of skirts and tube socks, my petite and athletic mother bounded over the front seat. She folded her arms around me. My tears paused long enough for her to reason with me.

"Now," she started slowly with a sensible question, "If you did die, wouldn't you like to go and live with Jesus?"

That question ignited a teachable moment. I forgot to resume crying while the wind and the rain beat down on the car. She gently explained that Jesus was knocking at the door of my heart. He wanted to come in and make my heart his home.

In a soothing voice that calmed the babies but only made sense to me, she promised that after my death Jesus would someday welcome me to live forever in mansions above.

He was in heaven now, she assured me, preparing a home for each of us who believe and receive him as Lord.

While the storm continued to pound us like a car wash, I yielded for the first time. Too young to understand the whole theology involved, I called upon the Lord according to Romans 10:13.

Was I "born again" in that storm? Probably, the answer is "yes".

I never looked back from that moment onward. I never feared death again.

Whatever happened spiritually, I was no longer alone. Jesus came into my heart and life, and he has been with me ever since.

Fear was gone. I knew from that moment on that "I am his, and he is mine." The spirit world opened. The Lord was walking with me. Jesus was dwelling in me. I first surrendered control of little life to God that moment. I called Jesus my Lord.

I Was Born Again as a Preschooler

You don't have to understand the theology involved to know that you belong to him. I knew he was in me, and I was in him. I didn't have to understand it all to believe it.

That's why not only children but even unlearned, ignorant adults can believe and be saved. In fact, even the mentally challenged can believe. My brother, who has been institutionalized all his life with a brain injury at birth, has believing faith.

"Faith believing" (the faith that saves the soul) is not a matter of intelligence; it is a matter of the will.

Over the years since that day, I have learned that "childhood conversions" like mine are not an uncommon experience. God gives even very young children opportunities to yield.

Some accept right away without any resistance. Some have moms and dads like mine who encourage belief even while their babies are still in the womb.

Many of my Christian friends also remember starting their spiritual journeys at three or four years of age. Preschoolers can have a lot of spiritual sensitivity.

In fact, at three years of age, I knew I was a sinner and in danger of death and judgment. That's why the storm terrified me so. Even at that young age, I knew that I was not ready to die.

Sin and shame and rebellion begin early as well. In fact, many criminals and sexual perverts testify that they first began yielding to iniquity and temptation very early in life. That's why many homosexuals testify that they cannot ever remember a time when they were not attracted to the same sex. We can be precocious in either *faith* or *unbelief,* in *obedience* or *disobedience.*

What if my mother had responded to my cries differently? What if instead, she had scolded me or slapped me into silence. That was common in the neighborhoods where we grew up.

What if she had shouted back at me, "You're not going to die, dummy. Look at what you're doing to your brothers!" or, "Shut up, stupid, or I'll really give you something to cry about!"

Thank God, she didn't. Thank God for spiritually minded adults like my mom. She could look into my young child's heart and respond with the love of God. I grew up in a home surrounded by the love of God—so it was much easier for me to yield early. Both my mom and dad were yielded ones, and they wordlessly modeled a life of believing faith.

Parents, take warning. You are more important than you will ever know in the spiritual development of your children. Big sisters, take note. Big brothers, pay heed. The children in your life will hear the calls for God if you will prepare them.

Which leads to my second baby step leading and preparing me for that night of prayer in Crowell Hall.

At Age Seven: I Make My Second Right Choice

A few years after accepting Jesus into my heart during that storm, back in my hometown of Chicago, I found myself in my dad's offices at Cook County Hospital. There, in the Fantus Clinic overlooking Louis Pasteur Park, I had my next epiphany.

I was probably around age seven or eight by then. My brothers and I were recklessly sliding around on the shiny marble floors in our stocking feet. Suddenly, a strange, musty smell drew me into a long storage closet. (This storeroom was a built-in "cloak room." All Victorian-era schools, offices, and hospitals had them back in those days.)

In my dad's office, it was called "the Bible room," and I was about to discover why.

On the enameled, steel shelves were neat bundles, wrapped in waxed Kraft paper and stacked high above my head. The smell that allured me into the room was wafting off those stacks. The air was filled with that strange smell, the intoxicating scents of printer's ink. The top bundle on each pile had been sliced open. The delicious aroma of freshly bound and printed books drew me deeper and deeper into the darkened room.

I think my lifelong love affair with Bibles and books began that day. (It makes me sorry for all the young people who only read books on their Kindles or similar devices!)

Curious, I climbed the stepladder to handle and started to open the various books. Often printed in two columns, the letters and the words fascinated me because they were so different from English. Each book seemed to be printed in a more exotic script than the one before. I didn't understand alphabets or written languages of course, but I was fascinated by the beauty of the bizarre characters.

Stamped names on the end labels gave me a little clue about each stack: Arabic, Burmese, Chinese, Croatian, French, German, Greek, Hebrew, Hindi, Japanese, Italian, Polish, Russian, Serbian, Spanish, Swedish, Tamil, Thai, Ukrainian, and Yiddish.

My dad the chaplain appeared.

"What are these funny-looking books?" I asked. "What kind of writing is this?"

Dad answered, "These are the Word of God in other languages. God has brought people here to this hospital from all over the world.

"When I visit them in the wards, many want to have the Bible in their own language. That's why we have New Testaments here in twenty-eight languages—the Lord loves everybody and wants them all to hear the truth in their own mother tongue."

Lightning struck my mind. God spoke all languages! The new idea exploded in my mind like a bomb. I felt the power of God's revelation emanating from those sacred books. The thought overwhelmed me; God is revealed in many languages—not just English. So, everyone could know His love, not just us.

The whole idea of language, speech, and alphabets gripped me. There were other scripts—others had God's word available in their written languages too! God understood and spoke other tongues. At that moment, I felt God's love calling me to him and to this work; I felt the call of the nations for the first time.

Suddenly I understood. I wanted everyone to have God's truth in their own tongues. God cared about all nations.

So Suddenly, I Was "Called to All"

That minute, I instantly wanted to take some Italian Bibles home to our neighbors, to Luke Deluge's dad from the old world ... to the Italian grandmothers all dressed in black, to the Sicilian and Russian babushkas—the grannies who could not understand my English.

The world opened up. That meant the family of Steve, the Jewish green grocer's son, could also read the Jewish Bible in Hebrew ... that Abdin and his Puerto Rican grandma could read in Spanish ... my deportee girlfriends Valentina and Senna from Ukraine could read too!

A great veil fell from my eyes that day. We lived off Taylor Street in Little Italy between Greek Town and Jew Town. My brothers and I thought we were the only blue-eyed "Protestant devils" in a sea of black-eyed, olive-skinned immigrants from Palermo and Syracuse.

I was a bullied, chubby, blond-haired heretic, an alien visitor on an otherwise Sicilian Catholic planet.

Beyond the safety of our Taylor Street neighborhood, the rest of Chicago's communities were strictly off limits. To my peers and me, all other neighborhoods were filled with dangerous gangs of African Americans, Chinese, Germans, Irish, Jews, Mexicans, Poles, Puerto Ricans, Serbs, and thirty-five other immigrant groups.

In this racially overcharged environment, everyone had an ethnic identity. And that identity was usually described in street slang—vile labels that today are considered degrading and unprintable. (None of us kids knew any other way to describe ourselves!)

Chicagoans defined ourselves ethnically and were gladly "redlined" into fifty Democratic wards and Catholic parishes. For me, growing up in Chicago's Little Italy was to accept that anyone not from Taylor Street was a mortal threat.

Life there was like a scene from the Broadway play *West Side Story*—gangs like the Jets and the Sharks existed, but they were defined in more derogatory, ethnic terms.

We were taught and we believed *all others* to be dangerously different people—we lived under the protection of our Sicilian godfathers, and it was comfortable. Outsiders spoke strange languages from strange places. They were divided from us mostly by the big boulevards and avenues, but also by invisible red lines we could not cross.

It our area, anything beyond Twelfth Street (Roosevelt Road) south was unsafe—and that was only four blocks away ... literally just seconds on the clanging Paulina Street car. (Yes, I was born and raised in the days of trolleys.) In the other direction, it was safe to ride all the way to Madison Avenue, but there things changed again ... and again at Grand, then at North Avenue, and then Milwaukee, Devon, and finally Howard Street.

Up until that moment in the Bible room at the Light Bearers office, I didn't understand why my Cornish, Scotch-English family lived where we did. I knew we were oddly different from everyone else at school and in the neighborhood.

I knew we didn't belong in our adopted neighborhood. We were so out of place—we were so all-American. So very, very white.

Now it all made perfect sense to me. God loved all peoples. We were sent there, as my father explained, to share that love supreme with them. God made them different colors, ethnicities, genders, and races for reasons too vast for me to understand—just like he made different flowers in the fields, birds in the air, and fishes in the sea.

But now I felt good about it. This was God's order of things—many tribes, tongues, nations and clans—and God loved them all. He had revealed his will to them in their own languages—just as he had to us in English.

I got ethnicity straight in my little head that day. God loved everybody, and therefore I understood that I must love them too. My dad was "called," and our family was "called" too. We were "called to all" and especially to our very Sicilian neighbors and all the nations that came to the Medical Center neighborhoods for care.

God was in the love business. He cared about the sick, the dying, and the injured at County Hospital no matter what language they spoke or where they came from. I knew he wanted me to love them too, and I yielded to that force. He is the love supreme—greater than our sin, guilt, shame, and rebellion.

From that moment, I no longer feared those different from me. I became a force for forgiveness and reconciliation in my neighborhood. I determined that I would learn to speak God's love in all their languages.

Without anyone directly telling me, I knew that God wanted me to be a peacemaker. Reconciliation and understanding became my hobby.

I thank God for a spiritual father who could share and live out this passion and vision before my eyes. He was a busy, preoccupied man supported by a wife cut from the same cloth. They were called to all, and they modeled it for me.

There was a final baby step I needed to take before I could be ready that night of prayer in Crowell Hall.

The Last Time "it" happened, I was 13.
I made my third right choice.

It was 1959 in Green Lake, Wisconsin at an August Youth for Christ camp for teenagers. The advertising called it a *"CampSpiration."* There, I would yield again. I made my third right choice. It was a choice that would eventually lead me to that India Prayer Band meeting at Moody.

That summer camp was where I set my spiritual GPS for the rest of my life. Vocationally, I submitted to God's will for me—to serve him. God lays out spiritual waypoints on the journey of life. That Friday night I surrendered all. Billy Bray's "who, where, when, how, and way" were now God's to control.

I was a high school freshman at Lane Tech on Chicago's northwest side. It was a sprawling, all-male, college-prep school, which was then focused on catching up with the Russians in the space race.

Although Lane was a science magnet school, it also had a big media program that featured a daily newspaper printed from hot metal type in our own print shops.

Rows of platen presses lined up like soldiers—their big inking disks shining with slick, rainbow colors. When I saw the print shops during a pre-enrollment school tour, I knew Lane was for me and I wanted to work on those machines.

I was already editor of my elementary school newspaper. I had done the tour of the *Chicago Sun Times/Daily News* plant as a seventh grader. I knew I wanted to major in journalism and broadcast the daily news.

My clever little mother offered to send me to this Youth for Christ camp as a one-week vacation break from my newsstand business. It was just a couple weeks before school restarted after my summer break.

My Mom's Sacrifice Pays Huge Spiritual Dividends

I was too young to understand her sacrifice—how much she had prayed and saved to send me to this camp. Where she got the money to send me I don't know, but I was shocked at the price tag and considered it an amazing gift. We still counted every dime of income. I was taking home ten to twelve dollars a week allowance, and *CampSpiration* was $128 or three months' pay.

I was instantly sold on camp when she casually mentioned it was coed, a word that sent chills down my spine. My hormones had just kicked in.

My mind had an adolescent fascination with the mystery of females and their soft, amazingly different bodies. The thought of being alone with some of those beguiling and mysterious creatures for a whole week was irresistible.

Growing up without sisters, I lived in an all-male world except for my tomboy mom, whom I treated more like a brother than a mother—just as one of the guys.

I invited a new friend from my freshman typing class to join me for this *CampSpiration*. A devout, orange-haired Irish Catholic, Dan O'Neal found a born-again girlfriend that week at camp. She was Shirley, and they double-dated with us when I started going steady later that fall with a sometimes naughty Swede from Waukegan.

However, the YFC camp had an agenda my mother "forgot" to mention. Between lots of food, sunshine, sports, and the lake—our camp director, a tall baritone named Dave Breese, offered a curriculum focused primarily on starting high school Bible clubs.

In fact, it was a Bible boot camp for baby-boomer teens.

We filled in blank outlines of subject matter in expensive three-ring binders with mimeographed pages and printed dividers. I rose to the challenge day after day and night after night. Some incredible, unseen genius had prepared those outlines and binders, and it changed my life forever.

Somebody had laid out my high school career for me. I was going to be a student missionary to Lane Tech.

Camp Curriculum Lays Out a High School Evangelism Plan

I loved having a plan for my high school career—and very cool speakers like Jay Kesler and Bruce Larson defined the spiritual needs of our generation.

I began to see my baby-boomer cohorts as a distinctive unreached people group while at that camp. I grew conscious that we were a unique generation destined to change the world for better or for worse.

Dave Breese was a very well-read, articulate Lane Tech alum. A philosopher and theologian, he had answers for the beatnik poets in Hyde Park and Rush Street coffee houses— to the sceptics at Loyola, Northwestern and the University of Illinois.

I was attracted to them. I was selling City Lights products by beat poets at my newsstands around the University of Illinois Medical Center campus. This was the first time I began to see that God had answers for the beats and our "hippie" generation.

Satan, the great enemy of our souls, has a way of inventing new art, music, philosophies, and counterfeit cultures adapted to the changing spiritual needs of each new generation. It's true today for Millennials, GenNext and GenAlpha—and will no doubt be true in the future when new student cultures evolve.

Breese amazed me because he had prepared the answers to the questions our generation was asking, and all delivered in his deep radio announcer voice.

And he was not the only YFC leader who had the answers to my adolescent questions. He hired a California club director named Stub McClaird, who later took me under his wing. He was followed by Ron and Karen Hutchcraft, MBI students whose guidance helped me become the club director for Chicagoland YFC before Jack Daniels took over for Dave Breese.

Finding My First Christian Mentors

Mentors like Ron and Karen were older, college-age role models that set the pace for my spiritual development. They shared answers with me out of their own life experiences. I needed alternate, Christian lifestyles to follow. I was searching for answers to the *Mad Men* advertising professionals, the Playboy and Cosmo Girl philosophies, the beat poets and the Beatles culture idols of the rock n roll world.

Thank God, they had the answers to the questions my voracious media-soaked mind had created.

I remember one black-and-white documentary film they showed that summer. It was titled *The Face of American Youth* from Ken Anderson at Gospel Films in Winona Lake, Indiana. As a young student journalist, it created a self-awareness in me I had never known before. The film awakened in my heart a sympathetic interest in my peers and their special needs for the first time. *YFC* and *His,* student magazines at the time, reinforced that message.

I had to find Christian media figures to pattern my life after.

Friday night, the final night, Jay Kessler laid out my life choices for me in a way I had never seen. He predicted that in the next five or six years I would probably find a wife, a career, a cause, and a purpose for living. Up until that moment, I was only vaguely aware that these kinds of events were about to happen.

However, I was never aware until that moment that I had choices in these matters and that God was interested in me and how I choose. Never in a million years would I have imagined that Green Lake was going to be such a strategic turning point.

Nor did I think I would be ambushed by the Holy Spirit so early in my life. That Friday night, at age thirteen, I came to my vocational crossroads.

I Heard My First International Call to All

Kessler didn't just preach a typical teen sermon of the day—to stay pure in high school, witness to your friends, and go to Bible school when you graduate. Instead, he gave a call to our generation, to the world, and to a life of sacrifice purposely directed to reach all nations.

I began to see that God has a purpose for all of us. We are not here by accident.

The altar call that night was so restrictive and focused on international needs that almost no one came up to the altar for prayer! As I remember, only Dan O'Neal and I finally walked forward. Not really having a clue to what it might mean, we gave our lives to Christ's service that night—to be missionaries at home or abroad.

The Holy Spirit presence was so real to us that we could not sleep. We spent the rest of the night in prayer and singing, walking the grounds while others slept in the cabins all around us. I can't remember exactly what we talked about or the vows and promises we made—but there were many. We went back to Lane Tech that fall not as students but as missionaries to the campus at Western and Addison.

Beyond that basic commitment, we also knew there could be "regions beyond" in our futures. For sure, there would be no Ivy League universities or space race labs for us.

The Cold War (or the many little hot wars like Vietnam) would not be for us either. The ISIS of our youth was global communism. It was as threatening to us then as the Islamic jihad is today. There will always be wars and rumors of wars predicted Christ and we accepted that violence would not be our way to serve.

Our career decisions had been made. Ahead would be Bible school and maybe seminary; after that, a life of service to God and man in church and missions.

Neither of us had a clue as to what our vows would mean. Nor had we really counted the costs of what lay ahead. The details didn't matter since we had given "our all" anyway. We had yielded to the creator. Our futures—in general and in the particulars—were now contracted to God and surrendered into his loving hands.

We had decided to follow Jesus. The issue was settled. Although we didn't fully understand it, we were also now fixed on a collision course with American culture, our own human desires, and all the spiritual forces of darkness.

I must pause here, again, to pay tribute to the Christian role models in my life. Youth leaders, pastors, visionaries, and even my Christian scout masters who encouraged me to win the God and Country Award and live straight. All of them had a part in forming me and preparing me for my coming Call to All in India.

And What about You? What's Your Backstory?

Your backstory is probably not at all like mine, except in one critical detail.

Every one of us must reach the same place I was in at Camp Green Lake on that Friday night. We must all reach a point where we choose to take up our own personal cross—to die to our own will—and decide to follow the will of the Lord Jesus instead:

- Unlike me, you may have been raised in a Buddhist, Communist, Hindu, or Muslim home. Perhaps you don't know what you are—you may be a typical modern student, a practicing secular-humanistic pagan progressive.
- Your mother, unlike mine, may not have had words of comfort for you in the storms of your life. You may not have heard the story of Jesus as savior and Lord from early childhood or opened the door of your heart to him as a preschooler. Yet to find the will of God at any age, you must submit to God. You must confess Jesus as your Lord like I did in the backseat of that car. *At some point, you must love God and choose to open the door of your heart and let him come in as master of the house.*
- Unlike me, you may have been raised in a hostile or even abusive culture. In a world of violence and greed and hatred. Maybe you lived in home where money was everything. Perhaps you were raised in a dysfunctional home or family.
- You may not have been raised by a wise father in a culture of loving outreach, service, forgiveness, reconciliation, and ethnic diversity. Yet this is no

excuse. At some point, you must also realize that God wills you to live a life of loving service to others. You must be willing to embrace a lifestyle of loving your neighbor as you love yourself ... and that means believing the Word of God and sharing it with others no matter who they are. *At some point, you must choose to love your neighbor as yourself.*

- Unlike me, you may not have had rich spiritual resources to help you grow in Christ. Perhaps you grew up where they persecuted believers in the Messiah, Christ Jesus of Nazareth. Or you may have been raised in a spiritually indifferent culture where faith was considered irrelevant.
- You may not have had a good church, fine pastors, excellent Sunday school teachers, youth leaders, camps, conferences, and counselors like I did. However, at some point you will be asked to join the called-out ones—to be baptized into his body by the Holy Spirit. The Lord wants you to be part of the living Body of Christ in your community, a called-out and separated people who will teach and preach and live out lives of righteousness and faith. *At some point, you must identify with God's people.*
- Or unlike me, you may have been raised in Christian rituals yet never been born again by the Spirit. You may have grown up in a deeply religious, nominally Christian home like John Wesley. He was baptized, catechized, confirmed, ordained, and sent to the mission field. He had studied well in the best seminaries and correctly practiced every liturgy and rubric in the Book of Common Prayer. He had piety but was never born again, and that finally happened one day long after he was ordained in the Anglican priesthood! There are many pastors, Sunday school teachers, and choir directors who are just as lost as the worst terrorist on death row—religious but still

facing condemnation and judgment from God at his great white throne. *At some point, you must be born again by the Spirit of the Lord.*

You don't have to make these kinds of decisions to follow Jesus, like I did, at an early age. You can make them at any point in your life. It is never too late.

Many respond to the early calls of God in their high school and college years, but you can do it at any time. You may be in the armed forces, college, prison, or a group home today. Maybe you are in a hospital or long-term recovery unit. Wherever you are, it is not too late to make the right choices with your life and will.

"For by grace are you saved through faith," says the Bible. "And this is not your own doing; it is the gift of God, not a result of works, so that no one may boast" (Ephesians 2:8–9).

"For everyone who calls on the name of the Lord will be saved" (Romans 10:13).

If you picked up this book to find and do the will of God, you can start right now. If you haven't yet surrendered yourself to him, then stop here and take this first and essential step.

You will never find the will of God until you are first born again of his Spirit. God is a spirit, and Jesus says he seeks those who worship him in Spirit and in truth.

So, what must you do to be saved? "If you confess with your mouth that Jesus is Lord and believe in your heart that God raised him from the dead, you will be saved" (Romans 10:9, ESV). Do it right now before you read another sentence. It is the first step to finding God's will for your life.

You can't hope to live the yielded life until you are born again.

I took that mature, adult decision to follow Christ wherever he would lead at age thirteen in Green Lake, Wisconsin. It was, for me, my so-called adult decision to surrender all. It finally led me into accepting his vocational call on my life.

Suddenly, Christ was not just *Lord*—he was *my Lord*. I was willing to conform my will to his just as he had conformed his will to his Father's will in heaven.

Suddenly, Christ was not just life—he was *my life*. I was hidden in him. I was now a member of his living body.

In my Bible on that hot August night, I remember writing my new life's verse on the flyleaf, "For me to live is Christ and to die is gain" (Philippines 1:21 KJV).

Although I didn't realize it yet on that Friday night, every day from that night on was drawing me closer to my appointment on the floor of Crowell Hall ... the next monumental step.

It was the first step in my response to God's call to the nations. I didn't say I would go overseas. I wasn't ready for that. However, I vowed to God that I would go wherever he sent me—even overseas.

That simple "yes" opened the door. It ended up in my viewing my high school as a mission field. It made going on short-term missions to Spain, Mexico, and Canada a no-brainer. And of course, when it came to that night in Crowell Hall, I was inclined to say "yes" again.

Chapter 3

Choices on the Calvary Road

> *For all that is in the world—the desires of the flesh and the desires of the eyes and the pride of life—is not from the Father but is from the world.*
> —1 John 2:16

But before I could go off to Europe and points beyond, there were still plenty of big, unresolved issues in my life. Simply announcing that I was going to the mission field did not automatically remove the idols in my heart or the killer barriers that were holding me back from the mission field.

Like the rich young ruler who came to Jesus, I sincerely wanted to be "all in" for the Lord, to take up my cross and follow him. However, like that youth, part of me still wanted it on my terms. I was not yet prepared for Jesus to ask me to sell all that I had and follow him! In other words, I hadn't yet counted the costs.

Like the king who went off to war without enrolling the troops he needed or the contractor who started building a tower without all the money in the bank, I was not equipped yet to face the consequences of my rather rash vows.

There were things, secret things in my heart, that I still wanted to keep for myself. Most of us don't realize how deeply compromised our souls are until we pretend to start following him on the Calvary Road. It begins with what we sincerely think is saying yes to the call, but if it is real, that yes is just the first of many. One yes leads to another.

The yielded life is a life of continuously saying yes to God.

Others may have been fooled by my zealous Christian life, but no one was more blind or deceived about these sin areas than me! My pride prevented me from seeing how enslaved I had become to my own fantasies.

A Love Supreme, His Love—Not Mine

How I wish I could have titled this chapter "A Love Supreme" instead of "Calvary Road."

I wish I could just say that my love for the Lord was so huge that everything was easy after that night on the floor in Crowell Hall.

I wish I could say I just turned my back on every sin that so easily beset me ... every weight that was dragging me down ... that my love for the Lord was so great that sacrifice was quick and painless.

However, to do so would be like putting cosmetics on a corpse. All that makeup would only make me appear as one of those old-fashioned plaster saints. You know what I mean, the kind you see in old churches. The phoniness would still show through.

But that's not the way it was—and not the way it is going to be for you either. Accepting the call means you must accept the sacrifice, hardship, and suffering that goes with it.

Love did win out, however—but it was his love, not mine.

Thank God for his grace. There is a love supreme at work in us; the Word of God is active and powerful as we voluntarily submit to it. You must put active faith into the Word of God, believing faith. I did get victory. I took the third step—waypoint three on the journey, and grace won out.

Flying at Warp Speed into Pitch Darkness

But at this moment in my spiritual walk, I was learning all this for the first time. And there was nothing gentle about the radical changes taking place in my life. I made a bold decision to follow Christ as a disciple in the ways he demands in the Gospels. Suddenly I felt like I was flying blind at warp speed into pitch darkness.

Most painful of all, I was being challenged by the very people whom I was sure would support me. I expected challenges from the world, the flesh, and the devil, but I didn't know most of these challenges would come through those I trusted.

I Faced an Avalanche of Changes

When my bosses, classmates, family, fiancée, friends, and teachers began to realize that I was serious about my decision to obey the Lord, quit school, and go full-time into missions, I faced an avalanche of very painful changes.

This is understandable. As I rejected their expectations for my life, my best friends and peers began to feel that I was rejecting them too. And in effect, that was happening both in the real world and virtual world of my mind.

The rejection came in eight stages:

FIRST, vocational doors began to close in my face. I was no longer welcome in the same places. Suddenly, even my Practical Christian Work assignments and service opportunities changed. And this was among pastors and Christian leaders! How much more does it happen for those in secular places of leadership and service in corporate business, government, in the military or on the university campus! What about those in the entertainment world, media/arts and music?

Up until my decision to obey the call, my weekends were spent as a youth pastor in a suburban parish of Chicago.

Called to All

In that church, the pastor and the parents of teens trusted me with the youth program. After I announced my plans to go overseas and began to challenge youth for missions, the atmosphere grew very cold. I was no longer a safe role model. Parents no longer wanted me "baby-sitting" their teens.

And the feelings were mutual. The calendar of youth rallies, hootenannies, films, and pizza parties no longer satisfied me. I wanted to challenge youth for service in the cities and to the nations. My assignment dissolved, and the senior pastor called me into his office and told me that he was asking Moody to search for a new "preacher boy" at the end of semester. Other pulpits and churches that once opened their doors to me closed in the same way. For most, my message was becoming too radical.

I finally ended up spending the last months of ministry that school year at Cook County Hospital leading teams of Moody students into the wards.

However, it was not all dark. Some encouraged me—especially my ministry supervisor at Moody, the director of what was then known as Practical Christian Work Department (PCW). Moody himself had formed it, and it was a required part of the curriculum like chapel services and missionary prayer bands.

C. Sumner Wemp understood the gravity of the choices I was facing and the impact it was making on my career. Yet, like my father, he accepted the leading of the Lord in my life without question. He constantly prayed with me, counseled, and defended me.

I learned then the power of an intentional mentor. Every Timothy or Titus needs a Paul in his life. Pastor Wemp became my Paul. Never miss an opportunity to stand with a disciple in times of testing and rejection. Encouragement is priceless. I don't think I would have gotten through this period in my life without Pastor Wemp. Only he, and a tiny handful of others, listened and understood my cries.

Second, companions changed. People began to disappear from my life and our dinner table at Moody—classmates, colleagues and personal friends dropped away. One by one, relationships with people I respected began to end. I was surrounded in Smith Hall by several bright young guys in the pastor's course, theological students who enjoyed debates and matching wits about Bible passages, church politics, doctrines, rituals, liturgy, Greek and Hebrew.

Suddenly, I lost interest in all that, and they started losing interest in me.

My future wasn't going to be in the established churches and communities in which they were destined to serve. It was then that I understood that following Christ is not a popularity contest. It is not about pleasing your peers, the church establishment, and the professional servants of the church. It is about obedience to the Lord's call.

Also, it is not about denominationalism, shared doctrinal worldviews, or religious experiences. I no longer felt an urgency to adopt and defend a personal systematic theology or to promote a label or logo. I realized that the academic ladder I was climbing was leaning against the wrong wall! It led to a place where the Lord was not calling me.

And how much more is this true for a student pursuing a traditional, secular education. Even if you stay in your field of study, it becomes a duty—no longer the primary passion of your life. Which leads me to my next point of change.

Third, my academic interests changed. The Lord had put me on a different path. The next semester, I changed majors and elected to take subjects off the beaten path—subjects more practical than the theology-driven load I had been carrying in the pastor's course.

I began to educate for my calling.

Most of my professors at first tried to reason with me, pleading with me to stay on the academic ladder. There are two big paths in Christian service. The narrow one follows Christ wherever he leads; the other broad way follows men and their formulas for ecclesiastical and professional success.

The pundit's advice was always some variation of "there will always be time for missions later—now stay put and just finish the pastor's course, get more degrees, find a good seminary, and a nice little church in a good denomination."

I knew that for me, this professional line of advice was from man and not from God. Developing a systematic theology, studying doctrines, and debating behaviors are endless; it was clear to me that I didn't need these things to preach or live out the gospel.

While Bible study is a lifetime duty, I had what I thought I needed to do the work of God in the gospels and church epistles. It was time for me to end my formal education. The Lord was calling. A few brave academics saw this and defended me.

Dean Broman stood beside me in the face of critics. He kept my eyes on Christ, as did Glenn Arnold in Communications, Paul Little and Walt Carlson at WMBI, Rosemary Turner in the Missions Department, and Fred Dickenson in Bible and Theology. They defended my search to follow Christ, even if it meant leaving without my diploma or degree. They encouraged me to follow Christ no matter what the cost.

As I went further along this path of academic disobedience, a strange thing happened. One by one, I started losing academic friends and champions among the faculty. I was going off the reservation, and it might hurt their careers to be seen with me. A polite distance began to develop, and that led to more communication failures, even confrontations and animosity. We were busy in different worlds, and my decision was putting me into another orbit. I started losing some of my best friends.

"You're committing academic suicide," said one professor to me, shaking his head in mixture of mocking respect and disappointment.

"If I've ever seen a candidate for martyrdom, it's you," he added, and not in an approving way.

Fourth, hearts were broken; romantic relationships changed. Now, nothing was more painful to me than the loss of my childhood sweetheart. She came from a strong Christian family and was devoted to the Lord—however, she was convinced that I could not be hearing from God.

How could I be dumping her? She was confused.

We had dated all through high school. She proudly wore my high school sweater and class ring around her neck. She was completely invested in me emotionally, and I in her.

I was the center of her universe, and she was the center of mine. Right up until the week before our scheduled marriage, she continued to push for the dream wedding, which she and her mom planned for us—but I knew was wrong.

However, in suburban Chicago during the late fifties and early sixties, you didn't put missions ahead of marriage. Putting me through college and seminary was her American dream—with the statistical 2.3 children to follow as soon as possible.

"Why can't you just serve the Lord here at home?" she asked in dismay. "God doesn't care where you go—there are many needs right here at home you know!"

I soon found from many counselors that it was not okay to take a young wife overseas—or for engaged couples to separate for two years at time, even to serve the Lord on different continents.

My insistence on going when the Lord was calling was about to cost me my fiancée. It broke not only her heart but the hearts of her mother, my mother, and both our families.

Even after I decided to call off the wedding, she remained in total denial—along with most of her family and friends. She stubbornly refused to even consider joining me. She was simply not called to that. At first, she insisted on waiting "until I saw how wrong I was ... until I got over this craziness."

Being a pastor's wife in a suburban parish was fine with her. Had I decided to stay in the United States, I think she would have been good in the manse, good in bed, and still my wife today.

Meanwhile, we were both racked by guilt and shame. We had already taken advantage of each other in a high-stakes game of emotional and sexual Russian roulette. We had selfishly used each other.

She was still willing to do or try anything to keep me in her life—even promise things I knew she couldn't fulfill or say things she really didn't believe.

Even after our broken vows and cancelled wedding, she followed me to Moody summer school in '65. More than once, she suggested we elope, still hoping that I would relent and stay in the United States.

Then one day, it was over. I received a neatly addressed package at my post office box. Inside was her engagement ring with a terse good-bye note. I knew how deeply she cherished this token of our now broken promises. This was final. I broke down and cried there in the lobby of the Merchandise Mart. For I too had secretly hoped for reconciliation. I was praying that she would yield to the call, joining me on the mission field—wherever that might be.

Fifth, a change at home—my family accepts my decision in quiet despair. I was the first in our family with plans to go onto college and seminary. My dad dreamed I would take over the Light Bearer's citywide chaplaincy program that he led. Yet he knew I was taking a fatal path. I was leaving the family farm—it was like giving up the family business.

Following the Lord into global missions was not possible if I was to fulfill his dreams for me.

At the time, institutional chaplaincy programs were changing, growing more professional and psychology based. A master's degree or equivalent was being required for almost any post in hospitals, jails, or other public institutions.

What's more ironic, I believed in ministry to the sick and imprisoned almost as much as my dad did. He had been grooming me and instilling his work ethic and passion in me for years. I also knew that the call to overseas missions was taking me away from his work, probably forever.

Dad was head Protestant chaplain at Cook County Hospital for twenty-nine years. He served on boards of other Light Bearer's programs at twenty-eight other public institutions in California, Illinois, Indiana, and Michigan—in hospitals, jails, nursing homes, sanatoriums, and halfway houses.

You didn't pass up a chance like this to take over your father's ministry. Not in the world of Chicago power politics. My dad was grooming me to become his assistant at the Light Bearers Association and the national director of our family's mission when I got tired of serving a suburban parish. He was praying for me to do *home missions*, not *foreign missions*. I was the apple of his eye, and he was terribly disappointed at my apparent lack of judgment.

To accept the idea that God was calling me overseas was hard on him in many ways. It broke my parents' hearts and dashed their hopes that I would at least stay in Chicago and complete the work they started.

This was a chance to have a powerful witness for Christ and break our family out of our blue-collar backgrounds. Only with a formal education, with earned multiple degrees, could my gentle father see me as having a valuable position in the ecumenical community.

He had paid an incredible price personally to get where he was, and he had what Chicagoans call clout. If I earned the degrees, he was sure he could make a way for me into Chicago's Irish world of politics and power.

Sixth, my mind changes—fantasy heroes turn to villains. For years, I had been cultivating secret sins and the worst kinds of lust. I loved television, theater, and movies—even though they were banned at Moody but tolerated in my home.

I loved all kinds of stories but especially those with an erotic edge. My years in the newsstand business had given me full access to the pornography of that period—not just the popular stag, romance and confession magazines but every kind of perversion.

Now, all this had to go. With King David, I prayed, "I will put no unclean thing before my eyes."

Living at the edge of a great university on the cusp of the coming 1970s sexual revolution, I had a front-row seat on the lurid world of "literary" erotica. This would eventually give way to the so-called "adult sophisticate" publishing world—what is now the global Internet porn industry. Studies show that most American Christian males, including many pastors today, are still entrapped in this Satanic net.

I had to yield up this idol along with all the others. In my case, I had developed an appetite for the demented world of Desclos (Paul Reage), Sacher-Masoch, and Sade. While I lacked courage and opportunity to put their vile desires into action, I had yielded to evil spirits, and my mind had become the devil's playpen.

These lusts were already virtual reality in my mind, and Satan was engineering my life to find moments and relationship where I could make them real if I wanted. It was only a matter of time if I stayed on the present impossible course. I didn't of course, instead I learned to "... Walk by the Spirit, and you will not gratify the desires of the flesh" (Galatians 5:16).

Not only did the Lord free me from this addiction, but my plans for a career in the media world were surrendered as well.

Seventh, hobbies and unholy career fantasies fade to black. Up until this point in my little drama, I had clung to the idea that somehow, I could follow the Lord and a news media career at the same time.

I learned to read before kindergarten on our living room floor, pouring over the *Chicago Daily News*. At Lane Tech, I had been feature editor of the *Lane Daily*. I also worked on the yearbook, the school magazine, and with hot lead in our print and Linotype shops. (This was before the world of digital communications!)

Of course, when I graduated to Moody, I did the same for the *Moody Student*—or any other media available. Upstairs at WMBI, we had the AP wire machine. I was hooked.

The truth is I was worshipping the world through media. I loved the world, and journalism gave me a legitimate "cover story" for my unhealthy curiosity. My nose for news was a respectable way to adore both power and powerful people.

The news business gave me an acceptable way to love all the things of the world—art, business, crime, entertainment, fashion, food, government, politics, religion, sports, and war. They were all fair game. They were on the "normal" daily menu in the media.

An ambition or dream can become an idol too, just as much as something you already possess or just covet. I was addicted to news and the people who made it long before there was an Internet. I was so addicted to this aspect of worldly power that it was my secret sin.

I had made a living selling newspapers, magazines, and mass-market paperbacks from age nine. During all those years, I read several newspapers a day, plus all the weekly news magazines – and everything else that crossed my sales counter.

Most of my heroes and role models were then media kingpins like Helen Gurley Brown (*Cosmopolitan*), Hugh Hefner (*Playboy*), John H. Johnson (*Ebony*, *Jet*), and Henry Luce (*Time/Life*). Seeing no way to reconcile a career in the news business with missions, I surrendered that ambition too.

Finally, I made the decision to put the Lord first in everything—even the so-called innocent things he was exposing in my heart. That somehow, someday I could be in the world but not of it was a lesson I would learn another day! At this point in my journey, the media had to go.

I was throwing the baby out with the bathwater of course. I didn't know then that the Lord would someday give my media career back to me—however, at the time, it was an idol. It had to go, and it did.

Eighth, the love of money had to go; my life turned from relaxed prosperity to joyful destitution. Which brings me to the matter of the family business. God blessed me and my frugal mother with a wonderful income for years, and I had started to trust it—and take it for granted. That had to go too. Through my high school years, I had gotten comfortable with the income from my newsstand business and the concession we ran for the Chicago Transit Authority (now the RTA).

First, we had one at the Polk Street El station at Medical Center on the Douglas Park Line and later at the nearby Coyne Electrical Institute. We sold papers on the streets and at the ubiquitous newsstands then on every Chicago corner.

We ran these businesses for nearly ten years—through my middle and high school years. My mom took over the business for me. Now, I was not going back to manage them.

So, at this point, my mother decided that if I was going overseas, it was time for her to retire and give up the business. My mom had kept me in pocket change for the last couple years, but that was now going to end as well.

"Do not lay up for yourselves treasures on earth," commands Jesus Christ, "where moth and rust destroy and where thieves break in and steal, but lay up for yourselves treasures in heaven, where neither moth nor rush destroys and where thieves do not break in and steal. For where your treasure is, there will your heart be also" (Matthew 6:19–21).

Turning over the financial control of my life to the Lord seemed easy at first but was now becoming more challenging by the day. The Lord was asking me to trust him fully for the first time in my life. Now my only source of income was an occasional missionary offering or donation from my growing prayer support team! Some money came in from door-to-door book sales, but all my regular sources of income were gone.

Mary Hid These Things in Her Heart

Back to the life of the Virgin Mary, I began now to understand the full impact of the angel's annunciation and her single-parent pregnancy better. I also began to understand why she stopped explaining herself.

No surprise the Bible tells us she hid these things in her heart! She had to trust God. What else could she do? What else could I do? Per Luke 2:19, "… Mary treasured up all these things, pondering them in her heart."

The gossips were having a field day. To the on-looking world, Mary was pregnant out of wedlock. The family and community did not get the angelic announcements. In fact, for years, Jesus was considered illegitimate, especially by his jealous critics—the Pharisees and Sadducees. They considered him born out of fornication, and they never let him forget it.

Whenever you step out in obedience to a heavenly vision or calling, the opposition comes in fast and furious. No one warned me what was going to happen. Since then, many have told me similar stories of the rejections that came after accepting the call of God.

"Your enemies will be right in your own household," says our Lord in the New Living Translation. This is from the dialogue in Matthew 10, which runs from verses 11 to 42.

No doubt Mary lived with this kind of opposition all her life. Just as the Lord Jesus did.

His paternity was always being questioned, just as it still is today by some unbelievers. The question is still, "How can God have a Son? How can Jesus Christ be the Son of God and the Son of Man? How could this man claim God to be his father?"

Much of this opposition was right in his face.

Now, it was in my face too—up close and personal! I was surprised at how strong the opposition was from those in my own household. Jesus Christ faced this too, from his own brothers, sisters, and neighbors.

He knew the pain of rejection, betrayal, gossip, and backbiting. In fact, his own village leaders tried to throw him off a cliff in Nazareth. That's why he warns us in advance that we too can expect persecution. In fact, he said you will be flogged, tortured, and opposed by worldly authorities—and even by religious folks!

Jesus warned in John 16:2 that some religious enemies will think they are doing God a favor by murdering us:

"They will put you out of the synagogues. Indeed, the hour is coming when whoever kills you will think he is offering service to God. And they will do these things because they have not known the Farther, nor me."

So, Mary didn't talk much; how could she? How does a pregnant teen explain that Angel Gabriel appeared and now, you're about to become an unwed mother? She could have been stoned to death. The more she said, the more she would be rejected.

And that's exactly how I felt too. God had called me overseas, but I could no longer explain it. I ran out of answers for my critics. I began to feel I was alone now with just the Lord Jesus. But that, by the way, is a very good place to be.

Chapter 4

A Love Supreme

So now faith, hope and love abide, these three; but the greatest of these is love.
—1 Corinthians 13:3

Because of my freshly broken engagement and cancelled marriage, George asked me to stay behind and proceed with a Summer That Counts door-to-door literature campaign I had planned for inner-city Chicago.

If I stayed stable, he promised, I would join the two-year training program in August after the summer blitz teams returned for school.

My bridges were all burned. I had quit school. I had forsaken all.

By now, I thought I knew for certain that I was going to India, but then George would not commit. My actual field assignment to India would not be decided until I finished training in England.

So, I understand even deeper how Mary felt. No wonder she sought refuge with Elizabeth. I was so glad when school ended and I could escape onto the summer mission in the housing projects on Chicago's South Side. It was much less stressful. I no longer had to avoid arguments and listen to reason from my astonished and unbelieving community. All the questions had been resolved in my mind. The Lord was calling me to overseas missions.

Hippies for Jesus, Door-to-Door on Chicago's South Side

My roommate and first faithful man, Steve Isham, joined me to recruit a biracial team to work that summer in the Robert Taylor Homes—and in other housing projects on the Near South Side.

With the help of Sumner Wemp at the PCW office, we lined up several big African American churches to host our team. They helped sponsor our community door-to-door outreaches, providing a place to sleep at night and to cook our meals as well.

Our team included African Americans and other OM'ers who couldn't raise support to go to Europe or stay for the full thirteen weeks. Included were at least two black students— Sylvester Jacobs and Pat Harris. We slept on church floors at night and walked door-to-door during the days.

Many South Side church youth joined us from the Older Boys and Girls Conference led by Leonard Harris and Donald Guest. (Both of whom went on to be prominent spiritual leaders in Chicago and San Francisco.)

We found many open doors. I was so relieved to be doing the work, and the Lord honored our outreach with miracle results. We saw much fruit—and it was such a relief to be away from the doubts and criticism of family, friends, church, and faculty.

George donated a ton of Send the Light books to us, including Billy Graham's *Peace with God* and *Seven Deadly Sins*. Ken Taylor at Tyndale House, who had recently released *The Living Bible,* donated books, as well as Moody Press. Mothers loved us when we offered them *The Bible in Pictures for Little Eyes*, a beautifully printed, full-color picture book. I sold hundreds of these rather expensive, hardbound books on the South Side.

What we lacked in experience we made up for in zeal. We were a strange lot, carrying book bags and taking sponge baths in church bathrooms; we began to look and smell weird.

I didn't know how much until one morning, after knocking on my first door, a teenager appeared. Ignoring me, he walked away, calling out to his mother.

"Mom, there's a hippie white boy to see you!"

In a few minutes, she had purchased *The Bible in Pictures for Little Eyes*, accepted my gospel tracts, and asked me to pray for her.

This kind of thing went on all day for weeks. At night, we held gospel meetings in our host's churches. It was a great start to what I then expected to be doing for the next couple years in India!

Martin Luther King, Stokley Carmichael, and Jessie Jackson were in Chicago that summer to organize Operation Breadbasket. Racial tensions were running high. So, we marched with Dr. King, did the Soldier's Field rally, and marched in Cicero.

I was even able to interview the social activist Saul Alinsky once but it was soon clear he didn't want born-again volunteers on his team.

He was organizing demonstrations in the black communities and trying to stir up street violence through the Chicago Freedom Movement. As much as Alinsky tried to instigate racial hatred and violence in 1965, I was thankful the predicted race riots did not occur that year.

It was a strange summer in which we felt loved, accepted, and safe.

We had very few racial incidents. People loved us and genuinely appreciated our courage and faith in their community. By the end of the summer, we had covered all the big housing projects and many neighborhoods.

We sold a truckload of books and saw more than enough funds come in to join the two-year OM team, which was leaving from New Jersey at the end of the summer. George said little to me that summer. He was busy in Europe.

I sent weekly reports, and I felt growing confidence from the OM leadership.

God Gives Me an OM Girlfriend, a Special Helper at Home

On my way to Europe, I spent a week in Harlem followed by a weekend with the family of a fellow Moody student in the suburbs of New York. She was in my class and was the nearest thing I had to being "my faithful woman." She would eventually follow my example and go overseas with Send the Light. She also joined an Operation Mobilization two-year team after graduation.

We vowed to pray for each other, and she was an enormous comfort and help to me then and in the next two years. She carried the torch for me at home and was an incredible gift from God. She launched my new career in Christian service by holding my prayer and support team together back in the United States.

When I was in India, she sent out beautifully typed monthly prayer letters and kept the prayer fires burning back at Moody. Later, she went on to work in the OM typing pool for George and was a great personal assistant to Greg Livingston in Beirut, Lebanon.

We secretly confessed our love, made forever promises, and said a tearful farewell at JFK Airport. Soon, I was flying off to Zaventem, Belgium, with Steve and George. Others were on board our flight for the OM two-year mission, including Steve's faithful man, Sylvester Jacobs.

The Trouble with You Is Pride

I met George in the waiting lounge at JFK, carrying a placard that read: "World Evangelism Now." George took it silently from my hands and grimly tossed it into a nearby trash can!

Asking me to sit with him during the flight, we talked face-to-face about India for the first time since our summer conference earlier that year at the Bible Church in Cicero, Illinois. Although we had written to each other about it several times—and George had previously challenged me to go there—he was now "still praying" about it.

"Do you know your problem?" asked George in a sarcastic New Jersey accent that sounded just like Lou Engle.

"The problem with you," he said knowingly, "is pride. Maybe we'll have to find a place for you working in the London warehouse. You're not ready for India."

I'm not sure if he was just teasing, but the jibe hit home. It hurt so much I couldn't speak. I tried to hold back my tears, but they came anyway.

"Why," I wondered bitterly, "would I make so many sacrifices and give up so much just to clean toilets in Forest Hill or work in the South London book warehouse?"

Looking back now, I can see that this self-pity was really my whining, undisciplined pride talking back!

Over the years since, I have come to realize that he was 100 percent right. At that moment, however, I couldn't see my pride. I was sharing in the suffering of Christ, though. I felt rejected, and I desperately wanted to be accepted. Through the pain, I knew I had done the right thing in obeying that call to forsake all and go.

I stared silently out the window of the cabin. We were having a kind of lovers' quarrel—a family feud. We stopped talking and gave each other the silent treatment.

I barely said anything the rest of the flight, and neither did George. Slowly, a wonderful peace overcame me. The Lord had called me to take up my cross, and now, more than ever, I had an assurance that it was to North India and Rajasthan.

The Thar Desert still called to me. Although I would see George again several times over the next couple months, India never came up again. My ultimate destination for the next two years was still officially undecided—yet I knew that somehow the Lord was in charge of my future service.

It wasn't really George's decision. God was taking me to India.

However, the Lord used George's remark to profoundly change my life. Pride really was my problem, and the Lord had used him to put the finger on something the Lord was dealing with—and will continue until the end of my life. Every mistake or wrong decision that I have ever made can somehow be linked to my sinful pride.

Our chartered flight landed in Brussels where I spent my first days in an old paper mill OM had rented in Zaventem. It served as the OM European headquarters and launching pad for summer blitzes and the two-year training program.

George disappeared when the plane landed, and I was now under OM discipline—a top-down, chain of command military model. Unquestioned obedience and submission to authority was the first rule of OM life in those days.

Waiting in Belgium

So, Steve and I stayed in Belgium to help with vehicle repair and training in the "lorry" workshops. It felt like a cross between a military base and a circus in winter quarters. The air crackled with potential energy building up to the next blitz.

Vehicles here were refitting for use in the two-year program under the direction of Frank Dietz. He was an American who served as kind of drill sergeant for our training—a master of two-word commands like "Send it," "Do it," or "Finish it!"

Gravelly voiced from years of street preaching and door-to-door book sales, he was my first impression of a toughened soldier of the cross. Trained in blitz evangelism and utterly dedicated to covering as much ground in a day as he could, he was a pockmarked bachelor. His very presence bespoke of holiness and total faith. He personified sold-out evangelism to me.

He loved to work, and for a few days, we tried to keep up with him in the motor pool, doing what we were told to do as best we could. Our un-calloused hands focused mostly on cleaning up the worn-out VW buses that had just returned from moving hundreds of student volunteers during the European Summer of Service.

Then one day, I saw for the first time the British moving vans—a fleet of seven-ton diesel monsters that had just been salvaged from the streets of London. Skilled volunteer mechanics from England and the States were being recruited to rebuild them to move a spiritual invasion force for Eurasia and beyond.

OM had just bought these WWII-era moving vans in England. They looked like big red circus wagons lined up for a parade—a clumsy-looking, oversized line of mobile boxes.

The grease monkeys had to cannibalize three or four vehicles to get enough parts to recreate one newly rebuilt edition. These were to be filled with spare parts, books, and tracts—transporting the new OM teams to bases in Afghanistan, Lebanon, India, Nepal, Pakistan, and Turkey. If I went to India, promised Frank, it would be in one of these.

They were huge, windowless boxes mounted on ten big wheels.

"Surely, they don't really expect anyone to go to India or Nepal in one of these old monsters," I thought. "Where are the seats?"

But before I could find out, we were ferried across the channel for training at the Forest Hills base in South London. Eventually we would be returned to Belgium for our assignments.

In the weeks of study and training that followed, we had amazing hours of discussion with Frances Schaeffer, Greg Livingston and other leaders including Frank Dietz and George. I was especially fascinated with Samuel Thomas—the humble national leader of India.

Francis Schaeffer: The Calm Eye in a Hurricane

I spent hours at the feet of Francis Schaeffer. This was before his classic book was published, *How Should We Then Live?* We were in fact, in fact, using mimeographed pages from the manuscript to guide our discussions.

His insights into art, media, the spirit our age, and the death of western culture gave me the keys to victory over evil in the spiritual battles that lay ahead.

For me, being in the presence of Schaeffer and our British Bible scholars was worth six years of University.

He had an amazing way of treating the "cultural cause of the day" sympathetically but not too seriously. Along with the seductive lyrics of the Beatles, my baby boomer generation faced moral questions orbiting around abortion, civil rights, communism, existentialism, liberation movements, feminism, racism and the sexual revolution.

The evils of our age were real. Millions were dying in the communist wars of liberation, but Frances Schaeffer remained calm in the face of the atom bomb, Auschwitz, genocide and the Nazi holocaust.

Like Christ, Schaeffer suffered agony in the face of false teaching—the modern-day leaven of Sadducees, Pharisees and Herodian's.

They were all serious threats to the gospel, just as the rise of Islamic Jihad is today. Yet Francis had a cool and detached way of seeing them, not as the media did – but as another natural manifestation of the human condition.

Today's controversies on campus, in politics or foreign relations would not faze him. We need another generation of Christian intellectuals to analyze the signs of our times as he did so well in the 1960's.

Like Jesus, he recognized the dangers in our sin-cursed societies, but understood it to be what it was – the convulsions of the damned who resist the love of God and his mercies. Like the Lord Jesus, Schaeffer never flinched or panicked. He knew Almighty God was in charge.

This human crisis would pass. That gave me the courage I needed to face the future unafraid. Thanks to Schaeffer, I was not surprised by the attacks of cultural and worldly enemies – and thank God, he helped me to not to take the headlines so seriously.

There will be wars and rumors of wars right to the end as Jesus predicted. There will be terrorism. Bullies and threats from the world. We need to face them unafraid but with love and caution. We have the good news; we have the answer.

Greg Livingston and the Secret of Multiplication

Greg Livingston, always a pragmatist, gave an incredible teaching from II Timothy 2:2 on "Finding Your Faithful Man." He successfully made it appear as the most important part of every mission.

I went to the altar that night, crying out in tears of agony and faith, believing God for my faithful man. Steve was similarly moved, and we started praying together in united faith every day for several months about this goal.

So now, I had a goal for India bigger than selling books and street preaching! My bottom line was leaving behind a faithful follower, a disciple of Christ wherever we were sent. We needed to find an indigenous leader to pour our lives into – someone who would take our "spiritual fire" and pass it onto others.

This teaching was the turning point in my preparation for India. It was nothing less than a divine appointment. The Holy Spirit used Greg Livingston to give me the most important redeeming practice of my coming ministry.

It could be the most important take-away in this book—the secret to success of almost any calling or assignment.

The concept was not exactly new to me. I had been very successfully mentored and discipled by Lew Williams at Moody, who was a disciple of George. I in turn had mentored Steve Islam and Steve had mentored Sylvester Jacobs. We were already doing it and now we had to do it in India.

What was new was the spiritual core of this method. Up until that night, I saw it as merely an organizing tactic; now I saw it as integral to unity of the church and to establishing the Kingdom of God on earth as it is in heaven.

Finding faithful men, starting with a faithful man, fitted into a grand scheme of things. This is the cornerstone of multiplication evangelism as well as church planting. This was the dynamic behind Barnabas and Paul and Mark and Timothy and Titus.

It was related to how the Lord Jesus followed his Father, choose the twelve and then the three—and how we the body in turn, have followed him throughout this age of grace. It was also the apostolic rationale of our "accountability" to Christ and of a loving, sacrificing Christ to his bride the church.

I began to see how mutual submission in human marriage modeled the unity of the whole enterprise and is essential to spiritual life including the birthing and raising children. Without mutual submission, there could be no fruitfulness or growth.

Still not fully understanding the concept of the body of Christ, I saw discipleship in the "faithful man" mentoring model of 2 Timothy 2:2 as the life-blood of the church, not evangelism as I had been brought up to believe.

Like a kid with a new toy, I was suddenly a "faithful man fanatic" – and it was all part of God's special plan for me at that point in my life.

"And what you have heard from me in the presence of many witnesses entrust to faithful men, who will be able to teach others also" (2 Timothy 2:2).

Without this understanding, my coming mission to India would have truly been a colossal failure.

Ever since, a vision for "the next generation" has remained an important part of my spiritual DNA, in my mind if not always in practice. When not well-practiced, little fruit remains.

Blitz Rajasthan

Meanwhile, I kept waiting for George to personally come up to me and give me my two-year assignment for the program. However, one morning I woke up to find him gone without even saying good-bye.

I was crushed. I felt betrayed.

Other team leaders were also loading their vans and lorries. Where was my team? Who would be my team leader? Where was I going? There were farewells, tears, and good-byes. Last-minute prayer circles joined hands before each assembled team left. As team after team had their own individual or personal D-Days over the next week, Steve and I were kept in the dark about our futures. We seemed forgotten. We were nobodies.

Yet we were kept very busy. We just helped Frank get everyone else off.

Had my posting not yet been determined?

Were we going to be working in the London warehouse after all?

We were packed and ready to go—with Frank finding lots of places for us to help. I tried to ask about our assignment, but he was fully occupied with the vehicles and brushed me off whenever I brought up the subject.

We hung in suspense. All the others seemed to be assigned. Frank was acting like a field marshal, handing out military style map cases containing the *carnet* (a kind of vehicle passport) as well as the other documents needed for each of the European vehicles to cross international borders.

I noticed that the girls' team for India was standing around in their newly tailored, super-modest Punjabis—a loosely fitted sheath worn over Punjabi trousers, pajamas. They were still not in their vans either. Then I understood as I saw the big red trucks for Iran, Iraq, and Turkey lining up near the girls. A kind of convoy was forming.

Finally, they left too. We weren't even with the Indian team. I was losing hope. Only one truck was left, "Big Red." With it was a handful of Arabs and others destined for the Muslim Middle East—virtual strangers to me.

That's when Frank Dietz finally called me into his office.

"Billy, you and Steve are going to India with me at least as far as Pakistan or Bombay. I'll train you along the way in Big Red. You'll lead a North India team but recruit in Kerala first."

So, that was it—just two or three sentences of instruction?

Then with a naughty smile, he handed me the map case for the seven-ton Bedford and barked out only two words of instruction, "Blitz Rajasthan!"

Chapter 5

Blitz Rajasthan 1966

Truly, truly, I say to you, unless a grain of wheat falls into the earth and dies, it remains alone; but if it dies, it bears much fruit.
—John 12:24

On that long overland drive to India, I was still obsessed with Greg Livingstone's teaching on making faithful men. By the time we reached Afghanistan, praying for "my man" often became the first prayer request each morning and last prayer every night.

I wanted desperately to do it like Jesus did. I began to study *The Making of the Twelve*, a book on how the Lord Jesus called and trained his twelve disciples. I longed to imitate his ways. Living in community. Teaching while working. Seeking unity and interdependence. Making myself available. Being a living example. Walking the talk.

"Whatever you do," implored Greg, "never do it alone. Find a faithful man and do it with him. Take your meals with him. Live with him. Discipleship is caught, not taught. You're not just preaching a sermon, selling a book, or winning a soul to Christ—you are also leaving someone behind who is trained to replace you, to multiply you."

So, I prayed for my faithful man in India, even though I had never met him. Like a single girl praying for Mr. Right to come along, I prayed for my chosen one in India. Multiplication, not addition, was the goal. The rule is to make disciples who make disciples who make disciples—to teach others who teach others.

Overland to India—Life on the Road

I also practiced making disciples along the way, trying to make short-term faithful men as we traveled! But I soon discovered that the bulky furniture van made a miserable, artificial schoolroom. Life on the road was not a natural disciple-making environment.

What worked for Jesus as he walked on the shores of Galilee did not seem to be quite the same now.

First, the noise made conversation almost impossible. Riding in that thirty by ten-foot box was like riding in a mobile prison. Pure torture. Solitary confinement on wheels.

Onward toward the Hindu Kush we drove. By taking turns at the wheel, we could keep going day and night.

Our Blitz North India team, along with our passengers, crawled slowly across France, Germany, Bulgaria, Yugoslavia, Turkey, Iran, Iraq, and finally into Afghanistan. Numbers dwindled as we dropped boys off in each country along the way. Our top speed was usually about 45–50 miles per hour!

Besides our bedrolls, we carried seven tons of cargo, including a million gospel tracts, cases of Bibles and books, cakes of raisins, bitter baker's chocolate, electronics, tins of peanut butter, and lots of spare parts.

Some of the cargo, like the chocolate and raisins, was sold along the way. The rest, especially the electronics, would be sold on the market when we reached India. We financed much of the trip by selling our personal tape recorders and cameras in India. However, most of the cargo was the gospel in the form of printed flat tracts—fliers meant to be given away.

We traveled and slept lying flat on top of the freight in a tiny crawl space below the roof. One window, opening into the cab, provided our sole source of natural light, although we had an opaque skylight. Standing was impossible—even sitting at the beginning. Later as we started to eat and sell-off the provisions, it became possible to sit up.

A fine dust slowly filled the cabin. Soon, we were caked in the abrasive grit. Like sandpaper, it rubbed our skins raw in every sweaty fold of flesh.

Thirst was a constant problem. To avoid water-borne disease and diarrhea, we only drank scalding hot tea at truck stops. The hours between those chai breaks seemed endless. We showered once a week when we checked into cheap hotels.

This seemed to go on forever until we were finally stopped in Afghanistan by a border war. India and Pakistan were fighting again in Kashmir, and so the Indo-Pak border was closed. While Frank spent a couple weeks figuring out a way around the fighting, we enjoyed Kabul. It was a pleasant break in a beautiful country.

Afghanistan was a lovely, peaceful country.

The capital city was then a famous waypoint on the "hippie trail" to India. Thousands of kids were enjoying Eastern religion, cheap accommodations and food—plus, of course, the open drug market for marijuana and narcotics of all kinds. It was "guncha galore" for the travelers—and the smell of the local hashish was everywhere the students gathered.

My First Deep Disappointment

It was on this long motor trip that I experienced the first big disappointment in my missionary career—me.

It seems that despite my miraculous calling, I was still me. My way. My pride. My family background. My Bible knowledge.

My sacrifices. My religious experiences. My rituals. My training and past successes. None of it mattered. I was just as much a sinner as when I started. In fact, more than ever.

Just having a spectacular call from the Lord did not change me a bit.

It didn't take much time in the back of that lorry to figure out that I was not the nice guy I thought I was—and certainly no super-saint.

Going to the mission field had not turned me into one of those saintly priests portrayed by Bing Crosby in classic Hollywood movies like *The Bells of St. Mary's*.

My high calling and mystical experience had not curbed my flesh at all. I was just as angry, lustful, proud, and selfish as always. My sin kept popping up again! Life in the real world was exposing my religious hypocrisy, and it was ugly.

When I wasn't driving, which was most of the time, I was locked into a cage with a bunch of other missionary youth whom I soon discovered were just as wicked as I was. After a few weeks, I could barely stand to be in the same room with them.

And the feeling was mutual. These were all leaders; every man believed God had called him—and called him to be the boss. No one, it seemed, was called to wash feet. No one was willing to take up Christ's towel and be a suffering servant to his fellow pilgrims on this journey.

Like the first apostles of Jesus, we had more than a little envy and jealousy for each other. We were at each other's throats constantly and missed a lot of chances to love one another!

It would sound nicer to write, "I found I had personality clashes with my peers," but it was much worse than that. When reading the gospels, I used to giggle at the petty jealousies and power struggles between Christ's disciples. Now I found myself doing the same things.

Worse, most of it was clearly my own fault! I discovered that I really was "the ugly American" I thought I would never be—and not only that, I was an ugly American with a terrible temper. When I didn't get my way, I pouted and complained and never gave up trying to manipulate the situation to my own advantage.

And I found that my American colleagues on the team were my biggest stumbling blocks. We Americans were the biggest bunch of gripers. Within those first few weeks, I got into long, stupid arguments about modes of baptism, Calvinism versus Armenism, eternal security, and missionary methods—St. Paul's or ours.

I began to especially despise the regional differences of my American colleagues and started finding fault with folks from every other culture and country on the team. Suddenly a Texas accent began to annoy me.

I found areas of pride and un-love within myself so awful and sinful that I couldn't even recognize my behavior. I did things I never thought I was capable of—I ruined my testimony again and again. Once, I angrily threw a cup of tea in the face of an Arab coworker who enjoyed teasing me.

Remorseful and disappointed with myself, I went to apologize to the Lebanese brother.

"Never mind, my dear American brother," he said with a straight face, "I was the same way before I came to Christ.

"You're lucky you didn't do that before I found the Lord—or to anyone in my country—back then I would have killed you. Now I can forgive you and go on."

In Kabul, we stayed with the legendary medical missionary Christy Wilson. Dr. Wilson was operating a famed eye hospital. He had managed to build the only Christian church allowed in the country—one eventually bulldozed by religious fanatics soon after we left.

Frank decided that that Steve and I would fly over the war in Pakistan on a flight from Kabul to Amritsar. There we would rendezvous with David Burder and Ray Eicher near the famous Sikh Golden Temple.

Meanwhile, Frank drove the lorry onto Karachi. There, fully loaded, it was lifted onto a Bombay-bound ship. I would come down by train and rendezvous with the truck in Mumbai. From there, we planned to drive it onto Kerala, recruiting the 1966 North India Boys Team—mostly at the Mar Thoma Annual Convention.

Our goal was to recruit South Indians from schools like Bharat Bible College and Hindustan Bible Institute who would join us for a "summer of service" in the most unreached parts of North India. The prime goal: to reach every village in Rajasthan no matter how hostile, no matter what the cost.

George and the Indian staff had arranged for us to start recruiting at the famed Maramon Church Convention on the dry, sandy river beds of the River Pampa in Kerala. There, an Evangelical Bishop had invited us to operate a huge bookstall on the grounds around our big truck.

Arriving in India, I meet my first spirit-filled Disciples of Christ

Landing in Amritsar, we were briefed and trained by Indian nationals. I was amazed at the humility of these brothers. They were the "living letters" Paul wrote about. Each succeeded in outdoing the other in service.

David Burder was the Barnabas, always looking for a way to help. Very dark and thin, he was a Tamil from South India but dedicated to reaching the Aryan people of the North.

Ray Eicher was born in India of Anglo-American heritage. He had so identified with his Indian homeland that he unconsciously treated me as a foreign visitor. This was unsettling since his white skin made me want to relate to him as an Anglo.

Although they were my teachers and seniors, both men unconsciously deferred to me as the new OM team leader for the North.

This was a left-over honor of colonialism I had neither earned nor deserved. In fact, up until this moment, I had not yet developed a consciousness of my own title, position or rank – after all, I was only 18 and couldn't speak a word of Hindi.

Both Dave and Ray were soft-spoken and sensitive. Never calling attention to themselves, they could handle the harshest and most antagonistic fanatics with gentle humor – and put up with my American arrogance as well. They had mastered "witnessing in the Indian way."

This style of evangelism was based on a respectful dialogue, usually started by the missionary, it gently answered questions. It made the case for Christianity without confrontation. Their speech was filled with parable-like references to culture, the human condition, observations and reference to the Scriptures, the Bhagavad-Gita and gurus.

They never shocked the culture. Although neither were native Punjabis, they made friends everywhere we went. They outfitted us with bilingual Hindi-English Bibles, dressed us in Kurtas and pajama bottoms, and presented us with Hindi primers. (Later, in South India, we would dress in Dhotis and dhoti shirts.)

We started to draw characters in Sanskrit using children's art books, but I was impatient and unwilling to learn Hindi from the very start. It was easy in the urban north; it was easy to find English speakers—a dangerous disincentive for me. I had not yet been out in the 600,000 Indian villages where only Hindi and eight hundred other native languages were spoken.

India has over 3000 Unreached People Groups (URG's) and everyone has its own language, dialect and culture!

The harshness of the overland journey was quickly forgotten. I was flattered to be the center of attention in India. Without realizing it, I soon found it comfortable to become a sahib—honored and served by the Indian team members.

After a couple weeks of daily training and memorizing phrase sheets, I felt prepared to evangelize India—although I didn't have a clue of what I was doing! My idea of evangelism was giving out tracts and, if there was time, sharing "The Roman Road to Salvation."

Whenever I found someone willing to listen, I flipped through my English/Hindi New Testament, where I had marked and underlined the key salvation verses in the book of Romans. Many were willing to listen politely. For those that weren't, I could usually bully them into accepting a track or hearing me sing a children's gospel chorus in English or simple Hindi.

But before I could really engage in much evangelism, I found myself on an express train from Delhi to Bombay. Big Red had arrived in Mumbai from Karachi and was waiting for me on the docks.

With steam and smoke pouring out from our coal-burning engine, we went speeding and whistling our way through the night like a fire-breathing dragon. India was positively fun for me—and the speeding trains cut through the countryside like rockets.

I had only been away from Big Red for a few weeks, but I missed it and longed to pick up the vehicle and drive south to recruit my boys.

Once back in the driver's seat, I reveled in the status the vehicle gave me wherever I went. Although we never had much money, I always had more than those around us—and as leader, I kept the purse. I quickly became very comfortable as the affluent, bossy, confident, and entitled American.

In England, Greg Livingston had solemnly warned us that we should not plan beyond our two-year assignments—and unless we reproduced a faithful man, those two years would be wasted.

The thought seemed ridiculous to me at that time. Surely this would never end. I would probably spend the rest of my life here. Hadn't God called me to India? I was riding high in the saddle, ready to win India to Christ. Now that I was here with the truck, I reasoned, the job was already half-done!

Have I mentioned that I still had a problem with pride? Well, I also had a problem with delusion. First, I was trusting in European technology and methodology.

Second, I was controlled by that traditional, nineteenth-century missionary vision that Rosemary Turner had instilled in me back at Moody. I saw this two-year assignment only as a prelude to a lifetime service.

In my ignorance and presumption, I assumed that my six-month tourist visa would undoubtedly be extended forever. I didn't realize that Colonialism was over; I was acting out a fantasy.

Yet, despite my self-confidence, for some reason, which I now know was the Holy Spirit, I was possessed with a nagging sense of urgency. The Lord was not letting me get comfortable with Ms. Turner's fantasy of India returning to the days of the British Raj.

I had to get busy. I had to find my faithful man—the one who would be able to teach others also.

How I Finally Found My Faithful Man

The first time I remember seeing skinny, barefoot Yohannachan was in Kerala. He was in the back of Big Red along with other local boys who were moving out in village evangelism. It was love at first sight for both of us.

Unable to pronounce his name, we shortened it to Yohan or Johan.

I held my breath enjoying a divine conviction that my prayers had been answered. I instantly chose him as my partner for door-to-door evangelism that morning. I held my breath and prayed as we worked, *"Could this skinny boy be the answer to my prayers?"*

He must have joined us on a temporarily basis at the Mar Thoma Convention. We took some of the local boys with us for a couple weeks of village outreach following the conference.

The two of us made a good team. We were openly and easily selling books door-to-door. With my white skin, it was easy for me to attract crowds and collect "char Anna" for a gospel pack. (In a plastic bag, we sold a Gospel of John, booklets and tracts for 25-pisa, then about 5 cents.)

I loved these huge India conferences. Attendances in the hundreds of thousands were routine. All the numbers were bigger in India! Although I was not a great preacher, teacher, or evangelist, I was usually given a seat of honor on the platform. I automatically became the de facto voice of the team and OM—and I loved being a big attraction.

Yohan was only fifteen. He clung to me, literally holding my hands and sometimes stroking my white arms. By then I was used to cloying attachments from the Indian brothers—but never as strongly as this young guy!

His actions were exaggerated—more like a 10-year old than a teenager.

He spoke no English, but we easily communicated without words. Yohan mirrored my every move. He was so teachable. He must be my faithful man.

The same zealous spirit of God was upon him as was in me. We shared the same passion for souls, for street preaching and for attracting crowds.

He was very, very bright. Much smarter than me. He learned new songs in a single hearing and mimicked me as I sang English children's songs in English to attract crowds.

I had a *Wordless Book* "flag" stitched up at a local tailor shop—four bars of color: black representing sin, red for the blood of Christ, white for our cleansed hearts, and gold for the streets of heaven.

We waved that flag overhead and sang the words in English:

> My heart was black with sin,
>   until the Savior came in.
> His precious blood, I know,

> has washed me white as snow.
> And in His Word, I'm told,
> > I'll walk the streets of gold.
> Oh wonderful, wonderful day,
> > He washed my sins away.

And as we sang that song every day, thousands stopped to see this tall white boy dressed in an Indian dhoti with my skinny, ninety-pound Indian sidekick.

I was willing to be a fool for Christ. My skin color and hair, Indian dress, and my antics on the back of the truck were drawing big crowds for the message—and I was pleased to make a spectacle of myself.

The way I wore my dhoti, the wraparound skirt of the south, brought gales of laughter everywhere I went. In fact, I could just about stand anywhere on the street and attract a crowd.

Learning to Become a Clown for Christ

The Indian brothers, when they saw me forsake my dignity, gained courage and bravado to stand up with me ... to sing ... shout ... testify ... and preach the word in Malayalam much better than I ever could in my best English.

And all this was easy in the friendly south, where they understood the speakers and wanted to take our literature home.

By the end of our first couple weeks on the training team, Yohan and I were closing and opening the day together in prayer ... and understanding each other's thoughts.

There was still some debate about his coming on the Rajasthan Blitz Team since he was underage—but he would turn sixteen while we were in the field, and we finally got the permissions we needed from Frank Dietz and Thomas Samuel, the humble Indian leader I first met in London. He had flown back and was now in charge.

Like me, Yohan had grown up in a Christian home with a pious, praying mother. He had been dedicated to missions while still in her womb. My mom had done the same for me. She gladly signed the required release letter and gave her permission for him to go with me.

Also, like me, there was bottled up inside him a wellspring of knowledge and spiritual power. He was a "chosen vessel" per Acts 9:15. So we started out building our team, planning and praying each day for North India.

Our oversized truck was a critical part of the mission. Big Red was a moving advertisement, fortress, hotel, and warehouse. In most village streets, it blocked traffic both ways!

We slept in and under it, preached from the tailgate, and "tract-bombed" pedestrians along crowded state highways. With the vehicle, we felt invincible. I felt I could drove our way in and out of whatever problems we encountered along the way.

Little Yohan loved being up there with me on the back of the truck and in the cab; it was our stage and platform. I would clown around and warm up the crowd, and he would take over when it came time to preach.

In Malayalam, he could sincerely preach with Holy Spirit power, capturing the crowds with his logic, conviction, and youthful purity.

He had an insatiable curiosity about words, songs, and the scriptures—and he was interested in every kind of technology and strategy. He realized that I was a showman and marketer of the gospel. He wanted to know how things worked and how I was thinking, even if it was hopelessly foreign and wrong. He was smart and questioned my ideas ... and he translated them into Indian culture.

We seemed to be able to read each other's minds—even when we couldn't communicate with words. I understood a question or doubt in his eyes and did my best to answer it or modify my behavior!

He learned words almost as fast as I read them and soon used my well-practiced "sales talk" phrases that I had first learned in Europe and the United States. I had adapted them to India. I could sell a children's book or gospel of John with just thirty-five to fifty words, usually just pointing to features and naming the price.

Many of the books on the truck were the same ones I had sold door-to-door back home on the South Side of Chicago, like Ken Taylor's *The Bible in Pictures for Little Eyes*.

In most cases, Yohan only had to hear a new word once, and he got it. We went door-to-door in his homeland of Kerala where many spoke English. Within days, he was speaking and mimicking whole sentences in English.

I'll never forget Yohan asking to see my American *biro*—the Indian word for a ballpoint men. It had a retractable point, the kind operated by a tiny spring coil. He was fascinated by it. Within minutes, Yohan had it unscrewed and in pieces on his dhoti. He had to learn everything about everything—how it was engineered, how it was used, the cost, and how to operate it.

He loved the pen so much I gave it to him and eventually my American shoes and wrist watch too. He soon had the watch open and was studying it with the same intensity as the ballpoint pen.

This is what I loved most about him; he absorbed knowledge like a sponge. Everything I knew I poured into him—he was an incredible answer to my prayers—and he soaked up my faith level too. He imitated me, and that is what Paul asked of his disciples back in 2 Timothy 2:2.

That's important. Remember the rule, "Like begets like." Although we were from different cultures, we were more alike than different. We were both called to apostolic service and Holy Spirit manifestation.

We shared some of the same spiritual gifts and callings. If you're gifted as a teacher, you will reproduce yourself in teachers. I had that gift. The same goes for the other gifts (pastor, prophet, evangelist, and apostle).

The other nine manifestations of the Holy Spirit are likewise stirred up through mentorship—and I could quickly pass along a vision for the manifestations of administration and faith.

I learned that whatever you are—be it a helper, healer, or giver—faithful men with the same gift will be attracted to you. It is a matter of being sensitive and proactive when you find one of them.

After a recruiting stop in Madras, we were ready to take the Rajasthan Blitz Team north and win Rajasthan for Christ—but first we were invited to visit Hebron in Andhra Pradesh, spending a couple weeks in prayer and preparation with Bakht Singh.

We were attending his great annual holy convocation, and I wanted to sell our truckload of books and recruit staff members.

Bakht Singh and the Local Churches of India

Singh was a spiritual hero to me. While at Moody, I had read his biography published by Bob Finley of International Students in Washington. Along with the writings of Watchman Nee, also published by Finley, he had formed my definitive idea of what a great national leader looked like.

George regularly quoted him and used his teachings as part of his own radical vision of discipleship and missions.

In fact, I went to India with the idea firmly planted in my mind that Bakht Singh had invited our team to come. He was supportive of George and the OM vision to mobilize South Indians to go north with the gospel. So, I went to Hebron fully expecting to be treated as a VIP, to be on platforms and seen visibly in leadership. How wrong I was.

First, there were no platforms. In fact, I recognized nothing that made me comfortable as a Western Christian, let alone as an American missionary. Tens of thousands of Indians were camped out, eating and sleeping under temporary tabernacles. These were wall-less tents or canopies.

There were no pews or furniture of any kind, nor pianos or Western musical instruments, choirs or ecclesiastical architecture. We ate with our fingers on the floor in the same big tent where we worshipped and slept. It was like a giant sleepover for Christ.

There was no special provision made for me as an American or foreigner. No privacy. No special food. No servants or staff. No recognition. No special position, place, or assignment.

In fact, at Hebron, I was treated for the first time in much the way we treat foreign visitors in American. I was a nobody. In fact, I wasn't even allowed to hide or sleep in my truck!

Confronted and Rebuked by Bakht Singh

First and above all else, Bakht Singh was a disciple of Christ. He studied and lived out the Word of God in everything he did. If it was in the Bible, he did it. If not, he didn't. His literal adherence to scripture baffled me. Theological and ecclesiastical language was scorned. He used Bible words to describe Bible teachings and practices.

He prayerfully sought the Lord's guidance in every decision, and he made decisions very slowly—at least by my American standards. Nothing was assumed. Like the Lord Jesus, he consulted God about every concern and plan. He was all about finding and doing the will of God.

He waited on God, and as an American, I had no time to wait on God. I was a man on a mission. The man with the plan. Chicago is proud to be the "city that works," and I was a Chicagoan to the core. Yet nothing I did seemed to work here, at least not the way it did back home.

I tried to put forth my ideas to him, but Bakht Singh had no time for the theories of foreign missionaries or their money and "improvements" on Indian ways of doing things. Western technology was forbidden—and just because it was alien.

What's more, his teaching against the carnality and wealth of Western churches and missions was not just talk. It was fun to read his mocking views on "church as theater" when I was a college student in Chicago. Suddenly it was different here in India where so many things cried out for justice and modernization, in a place where I longed for some of the essentials of American civilization.

I know this sounds anti-missionary, and the foreign mission establishment in India accused him of just that. But to him, he was not anti-missionary as much as pro-God, pro-India, pro-national, and super-realistic. Anything foreign or exotic was dangerous to him, which meant almost everything the Americans or British did.

Bakht Singh was not so much a nationalist, although he was that. He was more a pragmatist. He understood the cultural soul of his own people and the spirit of the age far better than most Indians—and all foreigners. He was the Christian version of Gandhi Ji, and in fact he moved among the poor, rural masses in much the same way as Mahatma Gandhi did.

He walked at an Indian pace as well, traveling on foot from village to village. He kept Indian time like a farmer watching the sun.

He appeared to ignore me and the team when we arrived. He kept us waiting while he prayed for guidance. I was deeply wounded and indignant at this. He was surrounded by a bodyguard of "helpers" who blocked my way and politely directed me to join the worship, which seemed to never end. There was continuous prayer in the tent of meeting.

Brother Singh knew we were there and would meet with me tomorrow, they promised. This went on for several days, and I was insulted.

He was no hypocrite. He had spoken against the churches he saw transplanted from the west as British "theater," including the Anglican Mass. None of it was here, this was indigenous worship.

He was against the clericalism, denominationalism, exploitation, and racism of the British missionaries. He longed for a truly indigenous church manifested in native song, preaching, and worship—and that is what I encountered for the first time in Hebron.

And I was utterly overwhelmed by what I saw. A people who could pray and preach and sing and fast as these people did put me to shame. I was humiliated, lacking all these spiritual virtues. They were healing the sick and raising the dead. What could my hucksterism and American marketing skills offer in the face of this spiritual power? Even before I talked face-to-face with Singh, I felt like packing up my bags and going home.

Two things troubled me deeply.

First, I could see no way that I could assimilate our methods with this church or find a way to be used here in this amazing atmosphere of devotion and love. I couldn't even unfold my legs after a couple hours of sitting on the ground in worship! I was only eighteen, but I needed help getting up like an old man.

Second, Bakht Singh was very negative on the entire blitz concept. I saw it as logical, pragmatic, and unstoppable. How could any illiterate, unreached village resist our traveling gospel show?

To me, there was just no other way to reach India but from the back of my big red lorry.

After keeping me waiting for several days to see him, refusing permission for us to sell our books, and insisting that we worship and pray and sing praises with them for three long nights—I was finally ushered into his presence.

I was not ready for his confrontational kindness and pity, his kind and patient way of addressing me as a loving parent with an errant child.

After hearing my basic vision for reaching Rajasthan, he was gentle but frank and unsparing in his criticism.

"Your blitz team concept would never fit" where I was going, he said. Even if it had been successful in Europe, it shocked Indian culture way too much. In fact, a more inappropriate and offensive tactic could not be chosen!

The high profile of the brightly painted British lorry and the rushing about of my foreign-led team was deeply offensive. The bull-horns, the door-to-door sales, the open-air meetings were just more of the same old thing all foreigners did.

It was a British invasion, not evangelism.

If I went into an unreached village with that truck and my team, I would spoil that area for the Gospel for a whole generation, he said sorrowfully.

"We will spend years undoing the damage of your visit," he said. "Perhaps the wrong impression will never be erased. The worst thing for an unreached village would be the arrival of your lorry."

Anti-Christians are already mobilizing against the OM team, he said.

"Islamic Jihadists and Hindu nationalists think you are an American spy sent by the CIA to re-establish colonialism."

Now, Bakht Singh could communicate with me clearly. He was highly educated in the West. He was a former international student who had traveled in North America and studied in Canada for years.

He had spoken in my hometown of Chicago and toured all our big American cities. He understood my American fascination with high-speed, efficient movement from village to village, mass distribution of literature, and open-air evangelism.

"Your way will incite riots and communal violence," he said. "You will turn ten thousand away from Christ for every one you win."

He suggested my team abandon the truck and use more biblical and less confrontational methods—the low-profile ones used by his gospel teams, who were known as God's Servants. They came and spent weeks or months in a village praying for the sick, doing miracles, preaching and teaching each night.

By the time they left the village, there was a church, and they would leave behind a pair of church-planting native missionaries to pastor it.

His methods were based on prayer, travel on foot from village to village, indigenous worship, segregation of the gatherings by gender, and 100 percent native language preaching, teaching, and worship songs. Signs and wonders accompanied the preaching of the gospel. One-on-one discipleship was the cornerstone of growth.

He was caste-conscious and in fact was sowing and reaping mostly among the Dalits—the pariahs of the land. I didn't give a thought to caste or even basic religious differences between Hindus and Muslims—and I hadn't even been in Rajasthan yet!

No Americans should speak or have platform roles, he insisted. (He didn't say it, but he didn't have to. Obviously, there was no starring role in this scenario for me or any other outsider!)

Our lack of native speakers on the teams would never work, he said, but in the first sign of encouragement, he offered to send along local preachers from his staff. These were his full-time helpers. These were men from the regions we had mapped out who had been working in Rajasthan for years.

They didn't just speak Hindi and Urdu, they spoke local dialects.

Little did I know it then, but this was all of God's grace. They were to become the reason for whatever success we were about to experience.

"But There Are No Churches in Rajasthan," I said.

However, I could not reconcile his counsel with my mandate. I had "my orders" from George and the OM leadership. What's more, we had a method that we believed in and that had been mastered in Europe.

I tried to talk with the authority and reason which I imagined George would use if he was here. "Why wouldn't it work here too?" I challenged.

"Couldn't God use modern methods?

"What's more, hadn't God sent me to India?" I quoted to him my misunderstanding of the great commission as presented in Matthew 28:18–20 and Acts 1:8. God had sent me, and that settled it in my mind.

I didn't say it to him, but I felt those verses meant that unless I as an American was leading the team, God's commands were not being fulfilled. Why was I here if not to go personally and lead the team? To personally preach and proclaim the gospel.

Again, I didn't say it. But I had the checkbook, the team, and the truck! We had a plan all worked out. We were going ahead anyway—at least I was going ahead. So, I was as polite and respectful as possible without slowing down.

I was young and stubborn. I would not take no for an answer, and he had agreed with George to host us. Singh saw my polite but passive resistance to him, and the larger power of the OM missionary machine that was behind me.

He seemed to back down a bit. So, I took that opportunity to press him with what I thought was the key argument that justified my use of forceful, modern methods of mass evangelism.

"But there are no churches in Rajasthan," I countered smugly. "Unless we go, there will be no one to share the gospel."

I had just made a fatal mistake due to my ignorance and blind faith in my own propaganda. He answered me with a gentle, knowing smile.

"But we have many churches in Rajasthan," he said simply.

I was devastated. An instant witness in my heart from the Holy Spirit confirmed that he must be telling the truth. I could not answer his simple words. If Singh said he had established churches there, then it had to be so.

After prayer, Singh mercifully sent along teams of his Servant Helpers to go with the OM team for the first couple months—but only in the villages and areas where he already had churches.

They set up an itinerary for the vehicle so that it went from one local church location to another, snaking our way from Kota Junction around the vast perimeter of the state and skirting the Great Thar Desert.

When we reached a town or village, we parked the truck instead of using it as a traveling platform. These Servant Helpers did the preaching and interpretation as needed, not only in Hindi and Urdu but in dozens of other local languages and dialects.

There were nearly five hundred languages spoken in Rajasthan! It was like just after the Tower of Babel. That one Indian state could have so many tongues was an amazing revelation to me.

I could not work in the local languages. And it was not just me—none of the South Indian team members could either! When it came to language and culture, they were as foreign as I was.

However, with the Bakht Singh helpers, we got to meet many fine local leaders who were living in harmony with their neighbors. We did make an impact for Christ.

Over the next few months, I fellowshipped with many of these assemblies and ministered with local Christian fellowships meeting in worship houses all over the state. True, there were still thousands of villages without a living witness, but the church was spreading everywhere among the Dalit outcastes.

In fact, it was much more organized than I realized. I was also stunned to find that some of Singh's missionary workers were getting aid directly from Bob Finley at the Aid to Indigenous Development Division at International Students in Washington, DC. It has since evolved into the Christian Aid Mission based in Charlottesville, Virginia.

Nobody back at Moody or at the Urbana Missions Conference ever told me that there was a growing church growth movement underway among the untouchable Dalit peoples—a population mostly ignored by the former British missionaries in Rajasthan.

There was no Joshua Project or global mapping back then.

And most shocking to me, these were indigenous churches! That was my whole argument for going to India. Rajasthan was supposed to be unreached—and of course millions of Hindus and Muslims were still in utter darkness. But I was stunned at my own ignorance. I realized that I had been totally blind and misinformed as to the reality on the ground.

Because there were no foreign missionaries in the state or American denominations, I had wrongly assumed there was no church! Because the old denominations and the church relics left by the British Raj were shutting down, I thought there has no spiritual movement. How wrong I was.

Finally, it was time for my "evangelistic mandate" to take over the team, because Singh's helpers would not do mass evangelism with us.

I insisted on going to all-Hindu and all-Muslim parts of the state, places where there were no Bakht Singh assemblies. His missionary workers could not join us.

When the Servant Helpers left, the nightmares began.

First, the culture and language problem was overwhelming. Although I had tracts and booklets in English and Hindi, the actual heart language was usually one of the five regional dialects of Rajasthani. To my surprise, Urdu was as popular as Hindi in many places. Everywhere there were Muslims! Why hadn't anybody told me that?

There are 489 people groups in the state with almost as many languages and dialects. The entire team spoke only Malayalam, Tamil, Telegu or English—the dominant languages of their south Indian homelands and British rule.

There were other cultural issues besides language. We were wearing South Indian dhotis and other garments. We were clearly visitors from another planet as far the locals were concerned. Not only couldn't our team members speak the language, it was almost impossible to capture a hearing or communicate.

We used Hindi phrase sheets for book sales. Some had a few words in Hindi, the official language in Rajasthan, but none of them could preach or speak it as a heart language. When you are preaching and teaching, you need to be more than just clear; you need to be persuasive. You had to speak from the heart to the heart.

Just because the South Indians were Indian nationals didn't mean they could communicate in the north. Cross-cultural communications were still a nightmare, and not just for me—the Indian brothers were having as much difficulty as I was. We had really misunderstood the communication barriers we would face.

India may be one country, but it is at least eight hundred nations.

Second, caste was another nightmare. I didn't realize how huge this satanic scheme was. It was often worse than the language barrier. There are 1,200 castes used to divide families and cultures.

Most Indians discriminate against each other along five major groupings—Brahmins, Kshatriyas, Vaisaya, Sudras, and Pariahs (i.e., Harijans or Dalits).

But when they mate, start families and businesses, or worship, many new barriers are raised—it's more than just priests, rulers, professions, laborers, and outcastes.

The Lord said to go and make disciples, teaching them the whole Bible! That means so much more than just proclaiming the gospel. It means intimately working with the new believers in their homes and villages. The Word of God must be applied into daily living.

I was devastated. Not only must a foreign apostolic worker in India must cross racial, political, language, and people-group barriers, you also must deal with caste. The family and churches were segregated by caste, even among the Christians who were themselves basically outcaste.

It suddenly dawned on me. I could never master this, even if I stayed on as a traditional missionary for a lifetime (which was practically illegal after Indian independence). Only indigenous evangelists, disciple makers, and church planters could do that. Only local missionaries of the same caste could plant churches.

You had to be one with the people to make disciples—in India, that meant in the same language group, people group, and caste. No wonder foreign missionaries had failed in four hundred years of tireless evangelism in Rajasthan. Only Indians could do this job.

Third, gender was a huge problem. Over half the population were women, most of them veiled and forbidden to talk with strangers—including all males. A man could never reach them. Only Indian women had a chance at this.

Of course, we had no women on the team. It was "harem" to greet a woman—forbidden to even be near them.

In other words, you couldn't even hand a tract to a woman without breaking a cultural taboo. They literally ran from us and hid in their houses.

Fourth, mass evangelism wasn't working. The population was not curious about the gospel, as I was led to believe, but deeply hostile, at least in public. When the Bakht Singh servant helpers left, I began driving the big red truck into hard-core Hindu and Muslim communities using our European hit-and-run Literature Team Blitz methods.

Almost immediately, as Bakht Singh predicted, riots and violence broke out. The police and paramilitary units began appearing wherever the truck went. I found myself being interviewed politely by district officers, state militia, and CID agents from the central government in Delhi.

Up until that time, I didn't even know there was a CID in India!

Later, I learned that it stood for the Central Intelligence Division, an equivalent of the FBI and CIA combined—and it was responsible for domestic national security. That meant protecting the country from dangerous, foreign elements. I was too young and naive to understand that a case was being made against me and Big Red because I was viewed as a security threat.

Our team was creating very expensive havoc in a state that had well-entrenched enemies of Christ firmly in power. The Hindu "RSS mafia" and Muslim "Klu Klux Klans" were tracking our every move. The central government in Delhi was having to do a lot of police work to keep the violence in check.

More and more people were warning me of bloodshed to come, including members of our own team.

One Dark Night in Udaipur

I began to understand that Bakht Singh was right. The very presence of the truck was causing violence, not just against Christians but between militant Hindus and Muslims. India's religious populations are at all times a bomb ready to explode.

India was then a powder keg ready to blow whenever the right match was struck—and it still is today.

We thought it was opposition to the gospel and Jesus Christ. While there was that of course, it wasn't true in small, private conversations. Most of the opposition was toward Big Red and what it symbolized. It was an invasive force.

I saw a pattern developing when we used the truck in rural outreach. The team would have only an hour or two on the ground in a new town before a mob began to gather. They had to work fast and relatively close to the lorry, ready to jump aboard as soon as a crowd started to form. Pulling the vehicle out quickly when the mob formed was becoming more and more dangerous.

Eventually I would injure or kill someone, which might prove fatal to me or team members. Indian mobs could take instant, vigilante justice. Sometimes the police could not stop them, even if they wanted to do so—and often, they are afraid to act.

I began to fear that I might accidentally run over somebody or even a cow when I was making an escape. I knew I couldn't stop if that happened. It seemed just as inevitable to me that sometime soon the truck would be overturned and set ablaze. Already, it was becoming common for gangs of thugs to burn the tracts and gospels we were distributing—often before our eyes.

Finally, one late night in Udaipur, my faithful man and I began to share what the Lord was saying to us separately.

This was a pivotal turning point in my Indian ministry and in Yohan's as well. It was the most important conversation I would ever have in India regarding tactics. That conversation would affect the lives of hundreds of millions of people in the decades to come.

Yohan took me aside and asked to join me on my walk. As we strolled past darkened, sleepy houses, he spoke to me in broken English. "Bakht Singh is right," he said. "We should not shock the culture. The lorry is bad. The tract blitz is foreign.

"We must work as Jesus did among the people using the New Testament way.

"I would love to come back here someday without the truck and just work house to house with the people and plant village churches."

We talked more. From then on, I agreed to basically hide in the cab of the truck as the Indians worked the streets—and move the truck to a rendezvous point out of sight. We decided I should not go out in streets for witnessing and stop preaching from the back of the truck. It was simply becoming too dangerous.

Things started going downhill quickly after that. I realized that I was no longer an asset to the team. The blitz would have to be dropped whether George wanted it or not. Our technique was turning more people against Christ than winning them.

The Sahib Turns Sadhu

That's when I decided to try something else. With Ray Eicher's advice, we went to Uttar Pradesh for Kumbh Mela, a huge religious festival that attracted twelve million souls to the Ganges River.

I was amazed to find that Hindus believed a holy dip in the River Ganga would forgive sins—just as do some Christian heretics. I was amazed to find that Hindus have a kind of baptism, or formal washing, just as Christians and Jews.

It fact, Hindu baptisms seemed quite like the Christian superstitions about baptismal regeneration—the ones I had learned as a child growing up in the Roman Catholic parishes of Little Italy.

At Kumbh Mela, I also first saw the Hindu holy men and started to think about trying evangelism as a saffron-robed evangelist.

"Why couldn't I become a traveling sadhu?" I asked myself. "Why couldn't a wandering Christian Sadhu gain this kind of respect and audience."

I secretly decided that after the Mela ended, when we were scheduled to travel to Bihar, I would leave the team and try this.

It was an idea that nearly killed me and practically ended my first mission to India.

Chapter 6

When "Plan A" Fails

Teacher, do you not care that we are perishing?
—Mark 4:37

"No!" I screamed out to God as the police confiscated my passport in Calcutta. Could it be that my mission to India was going to end here after only thirteen months? Was I going to spend my last days jailed in an immigration lock-up?

"They can't do this to me," I thought. "I'm an American!"

What about my faithful man, Yohan?

What about the 600,000 unreached villages?

What about the millions of lost souls?

What about my calling to India?

"No, God," I cried silently. "This can't be. Why would you do this to me? I thought I was safe in your hands—called to Rajasthan."

All the prayers, travel, planning, and work. Was it going to end up here, in failure? In jail?

Those were the questions I was soon about to face in microscopic detail.

I didn't know it then, but my work at the Kumba Mela in Uttar Pradesh was the beginning of the end for my first mission to India.

It was peaceful enough after the growing violence we had faced from the fanatical anti-Christians in Rajasthan. The militant RSS nationalists were not organized at this giant, peaceful festival for some reason—probably because they couldn't believe that the Indian believers would use this event to proclaim freedom from demons and idols.

But maybe it was because we were a little more culturally aware at this huge religious event that had attracted so many millions of Hindu pilgrims.

Although I was tempted by the millions of souls that passed by Big Red, we did not use the lorry for preaching or singing the gospel in mass evangelism. I didn't know what to expect, so Johan and I decided to use it just as a literature base and mobile home for the team at night.

Soon, scores of other young evangelists from all over India joined us, and the strategy was low-profile literature distribution and one-on-one witnessing encounters.

We were soon giving out gospel tracts by the hundreds of thousands but not doing anything that might provoke the crowds to violence. But as it turned out, our fears were groundless. There was a tolerant, friendly spirit, and the Hindu masses were curious and polite.

In these vast multitudes, I could just stand around, and students would flock around me. Intellectuals who wanted to practice English and talk came up to me. I enjoyed an endless stream of interesting conversations.

Indians were interested in the gospel if approached gently.

More than once, I found that some of the "seekers" had an unusual interest in my name, address, passport, and other details about me and the team. I didn't give this much thought at the time since I had gotten used to embarrassingly personal questions.

Only much later did I begin to see a pattern in this line of inquiry, and so at the time, I blithely answered every question. Little did I understand that I was the subject of a serious investigation.

Was This a Way I Could Be Effective in India?

Away from crowds and the gospel team, in a teashop alone, I could sometimes communicate and carry on long, spiritual discussions. In fact, I sold our highest-priced books to these thinkers, including hardbound New Testaments.

There was a real spiritual hunger in India. Both Muslims and Hindus are very interested in Jesus Christ when approached one-on-one. This made me think. Was there a better way? Could I be more effective if I abandoned the truck, the blitz, the militant street preaching?

Everywhere at Kumbh Mela I saw saffron-robed holy men—thousands of them. In fact, there was an army of Hindu teachers, yoga practitioners, and gurus. They seemed to attract adoring crowds, either by their public display of puja, yoga, or occasionally by public speaking.

This gave me an idea. If I somehow could join this saffron army of religious pundits, might I somehow be admitted to the ranks of Indian holy men—might I as a foreigner be respected as a Hindustani would? Could a white guru succeed?

Perhaps, I reasoned, I should leave the team and travel as a wandering sadhu or religious teacher, initiating what I thought would be a more traditionally Indian way of evangelism. I could see the sadhus and fakirs attracting great attention and respect.

This was a perfect time to try the idea since we had another driver on the team.

So, the idea, once impregnated, began to gestate in my head. It was an idea that even I knew was so foolish that I feared to share it with anyone—not even my faithful man—for I was certain he would feel it ridiculous.

Eventually, I secretly decided that when we got to Poona in Bihar, our next destination, I would abandon the team and become a sadhu, a holy mendicant—begging for food and traveling alone to preach and teach the Christian Gospel. I imagined that I would witness to individuals and be accepted, like I was doing here in the Kumbh Mela.

This turned out to be more than just a painful lesson in how ignorant I was of India culture. It was a disaster that led me close to starvation and sickness. Instead of acceptance, I found myself despised and rejected everywhere—and most especially in the villages. Once I started walking in rural India, it was like I was on a different planet.

Most of all, I couldn't find anyone to speak English! Never had I realized how huge the language barrier was. I had seriously misread the customs and the role of Sadhus. I lapsed in culture shock.

A Crazy American, Starving and Despised

Most Indians thought I was insane. Why would a rich foreigner go walking around the villages alone in a dhoti and chapels?

"How did Mahatma Gandhi do it?" I wondered. Soon I didn't even have my sandals. I was barefoot, and the souls of my feet began to blister and crack.

Already weak, I began to starve and soon fell sick. I lost forty pounds on this adventure, and back then I didn't have forty pounds to lose! By the mercy of God, a youthful Assemblies of God church planter found me begging on the street and took me into his one-room apartment.

When he found out I was with OM, he sent a telegram to the OM headquarters in Hyderabad for help. A special "search and rescue" party was formed to fetch me south for our annual OM missionary conference in 1966.

(This missionary meeting was restricted to just expats from Europe and the United States since at that time, the "nationals" were not considered missionaries yet. They couldn't be missionaries, it was reasoned by the legalists, because they were not doing cross-cultural evangelism!)

There, at the conference, I was ridiculed both publicly and privately. My sensitive pride, already in tatters, was hurt even worse. I was publicly scolded and ridiculed by George. Thoroughly disciplined and humiliated, he gave me money and sent me off to shave my beard and get a haircut before rejoining the conference. I was very depressed.

My European peers applauded with laughter when I came back into the room–nearly bald.

This shamming compounded my self-condemnation and worsened my culture shock. Still sick and distressed from my trials, I was given time off to recover at headquarters.

I was not reassigned to my leadership role on the North India Boys Team either. In fact, I never saw my faithful-man Johan again—not on that trip.

Ray Eicher and David Burder took over my role in the north, and I'm not sure who was appointed new driver for the big red lorry that had been my platform for the last ten months.

The idea of blitzing Rajasthan or North India appeared to be a failure, at least to me. Although I can't remember any public acknowledgment, but it seemed that the use of the blitz trucks for mass evangelism was put on hold temporarily.

In fact, I argued with George about the role of any open evangelistic work by foreigners in India, suggesting that we expats should be used behind the scenes in the future. In the north, I said, I believe Bakht Singh is right. Our presence was doing more harm than good.

Perhaps I could do PR work with the news media or urban elites? Maybe we could start broadcasting? Maybe I could start an advertising, publishing, or media ministry? This was not a strategy anywhere in OM at the time—and quite outside the box. We were a literature distribution mission.

Before anything could be resolved, we ran out of time. The whole question was left for later since George had to leave India right after the conference. I felt very abandoned.

It took a couple weeks for Steve Isham and the girls' base team to nurse me back to health. Not sure what to do next,

Steve joined up with me again, and we were sent back north to Kolkata, then still known as Calcutta. We planned to do street work and renew our visas in that huge Bengali "city of joy"—an amazing misnomer.

On the train, Steve and I began to secretly talk about leaving OM in hushed whispers. He wanted to go down to Australia to visit his parents. But I was certain that God was not through with me yet. I wanted to stay in India and couldn't believe that God had brought me all this way for nothing.

At that time, it was beginning to seem like the most futile, fruitless, and stupid thing I had ever done ... but I wasn't ready to give up. I clung to my call—or what was left of it.

Perhaps, I agreed, we should go together and raise up a new support team in Australia that would send us back to New Delhi to start a ministry in the media and the arts. Francis Schaeffer had ignited a fire for the arts in both our hearts.

By now I was angry at God, at the mission, at India, the team, and at myself. I seemed to be a total failure. I had lost contact with Yohan, and I didn't even know where the team was. Everything seemed to be lost. I kept playing this record repeatedly in my head. Over and over, the questions ran:

What would I do now?

How would I live? Where would I go? What would I do?

However, the decision would not to be ours to make. The Indian Foreign Ministry and CID had other plans. Indian immigration had steadily built a case against me based on field reports from Rajasthan and Uttar Pradesh.

When I tried to renew my visa, my name came up on their watch list.

After a few questions about my work in Rajasthan—where I had been and what I had been doing—they knew they had their suspect positively identified. I was detained and taken into custody. The trap had sprung. My passport was confiscated, and the American consulate was called.

An Angel from the American Consulate?

After a few hours in detention, the American counsel showed up at the police station. Two men appeared; I thought both were from the American consulate. One was an older man in a seersucker, tropical suit. He was obviously a career diplomat.

Nearby, a younger Ivy League type guy stood. He looked maybe thirty. Very athletic. Unusually tall. Muscular. Strong. He was very out of place. More like a soldier but dressed in a sharp, modern suit.

The older man ignored the younger and began to meet with the immigration officers. He went about his business as if the young athlete was not even present.

Several Indian officers appeared with a lot of polished brass to meet with the older American official and the district officer—the senior Indian in charge. They were obviously going over my case while I sat on a bench maybe fifty feet away.

Finally, the tall, athletic-looking man came over and sat beside me.

"Do you know what is happening?" he asked as I stared at his beautiful sports jacket and tailored shirt. It was pastel with had button-down, winged collars. He wore the thin, fashionable necktie that was standard in 1966.

Without waiting for me, he answered his own question.

"The Indian government is refusing to renew your tourist visa because of your missionary work," he explained. "They think you have misrepresented yourself. They have confiscated your passport. You are about to overstay your visa. You are now persona non-grata and will be deported.

"But don't be afraid. They won't hurt you. God has given you favor."

With that explanation, he handed me a printed business card. He pointed at the name printed on it, whom I will call Ricardo Negro for the sake of this story.

Plus, I think he gave me a twenty-dollar bill—a lot of money to me, more than enough to live for a week. I was thrilled. I had not seen American money in over a year. It almost made me homesick just to feel it. I knew it would exchange at a high rate on the street—it was, to me, like $1,000.

"When you get to Bangkok, go straight to Ricardo Negro at the American embassy. He is expecting you."

"But I'm not going to Bangkok," I said.

"Yes, you are," he said. "That's where they are sending you."

Then I looked up, and he was gone.

In retrospect, I think that was my first-ever angel visitation—at least the first one I can remember. It was totally miraculous and inexplicable. Was he an angel or CIA? I'll never know for sure.

Whoever he was, the Ivy League athlete in the pastel pinstripe was right. I was only detained, not officially booked, and I did not have to go to jail. I was eventually paroled on my own recognizance but had to report in daily at the district office police station. I was given twenty-one days to find some money and leave India for good.

The immigration police kept my passport and promised to give it back to me once I was on the plane.

Then the other American came out.

"You're a disgrace," he scolded me. "You lied to get your visa. Some Christian you are. You've created all kinds of trouble here. They're watching you. You born-again Jesus freaks are wasting your time here in India. Are you doing drugs? Are you clean now?"

"I never do drugs," I said.

"Well don't start," he continued. "Check in with the police every day and just get out of this country as fast as you can. If you don't, it's jail for you.

"Here's my card. If you want me to call your parents, I will."

I did want him to call. And I assume he did, but I never heard from them. In fact, I never saw that diplomat again.

There were no cell phones in those days. No way for them to get in touch with me.

"You're staying at Carey Baptist Church," he commented with a knowing smugness. "That's good."

Not satisfied, he continued to berate me, "Don't you know it's illegal to do missionary work here? Why aren't you fighting in Vietnam anyway? You're a disgrace. You belong in the army. As an American, I'm ashamed of you. You have no business here in the country."

How Could God Allow This?

I was stunned. At first, I just couldn't believe how awful things had gone for me in India. If God was sovereign over all things, and I was safely in his hands, and he sent me here, how could he have let this happen to me?

"Why would God send me into a place of suffering and rejection and pain like this?" I asked myself a thousand times.

Here I was, stranded on the streets of Calcutta with nothing but pocket change and a little charity from a guy who never gave me his name. I was at the lowest, most desperate point in my life. I was going to be kicked out of the country and had barely escaped jail!

What would happen to my faithful man, Johan? I had been given only about ten months to disciple him. Would I ever see him again?

What about the lost millions in Rajasthan? What about the others throughout North India? In Pakistan and Afghanistan? Would they be sent to hell without hearing of God's love and redemption? What about the 600,000 unreached villages?

I had failed in my mission. I was so ashamed. I had made a fool of myself. The Indians didn't want me—and not just the Hindus and Muslims but even the Christians. The local churches didn't want me.

OM apparently didn't want me either, or at least they didn't have a place for me. I hadn't received a single letter from my OM girlfriend and devoted advocate back in Chicago. Had she given up on me? What about the secret vows we had made?

There was no word from George—the one most responsible for my being here, at least from a human perspective.

And of course, there was no word from my parents. From the States. From my prayer team. The Indians had confiscated my passport, and without it, I felt like I had lost my identity. I was a nonperson. An unwanted alien. I was homeless and didn't even have an address to get mail. How could anybody contact me even if they wanted to do so?

Remember, there was no email or PCs in those days. Telegrams and airmail were the fastest ways normal people communicated. A phone call to the United States cost a fortune. Certainly, much more than I had in my pocket.

At least I wasn't in jail, not yet—not for twenty-one days! How would I live? How would I get an air ticket?

"Yes, you're totally broke," said a pitying, demonic voice, "God has abandoned you. He brought you here, and now he's left you. This is what always happens when you put your faith in Jesus.

"Where are his precious promises now?" taunted the little voices in my head.

Just as I was about to agree, I recognized the hand of Satan. Those were little devil voices speaking to me—tempting me.

"That's a lie," I answered out loud. As bad as things appeared to be, I suddenly remembered all the miracles of the past. The devil had overplayed his hand.

"Wait a minute," I said. "God had always delivered me. He has always kept his Word to me! His precious promises have always come to pass."

It was clear to me then that the enemy was speaking. I wasn't going to agree with him. A great peace flooded my soul. Somehow, I knew deep in my spirit that I was safe in the hands of the Lord and that God would never fail me. I didn't understand what was going on, but surely the Lord would rescue me.

And of course, in reality—things were not nearly as bad as they appeared. People around the world were indeed praying for me.

The truth is always this. God knew exactly where I was—and he knows where you are too at every point in your life. His eye is always upon us. Our names are written in the palms of his hands. He keeps our tears in his bottle.

Don't Be Surprised When Storms Strike Your Life

Would Christ deliberately send me into a deadly storm? Had he not done so by sending me to Rajasthan, the center of the anti-Christian hate belt?

But if he had done so, and it seemed to be certain he had, was this a lesson? That was the first question I asked.

I hadn't expected suffering to come as part of my call, and it had no place in my youthful thinking. Yet suffering has many purposes in the Christian's life. Whole books and libraries have been written on this subject.

The Bible says that suffering was part of God's plan for our Lord Jesus! It taught him obedience. It led to our redemption, and it is a privilege for the Christian to enter the fellowship of his sufferings!

Yes, through suffering with Christ, we bring salvation to all nations.

In fact, Hebrews 12:2 says that we should be "looking to Jesus, the founder and perfector of our faith, who for the joy that was set before him endured the cross, despising the shame, and is seated at the right hand of the throne of God."

But there is another reason for suffering—another explanation for the storms in our lives. It is for our teaching and training.

Hebrews 12:5 says, "My son, do not regard lightly the discipline of the Lord, nor be weary when reproved by him. For the Lord disciplines the one he loves and chastises every son whom he receives ..."

Verse 11 explains the reason, "For the moment all discipline seems painful rather than pleasant, but later it yields the peaceful fruit of righteousness to those who have been trained by it."

Sometimes a storm is for chastisement, for correction. In fact, the book of Proverbs says we should love discipline. It is a major theme of the book, Chapter 12:1 explains the mystery, "Whosoever loves discipline loves knowledge, but he who hates reproof is stupid."

So, we should welcome storms. At least look for the lessons in them. In this case, God had brought me all the way to India to teach me a lesson ... and not just for me! Was it also a lesson for Johan? For our OM India leaders? For Indian missions in general? For George? For the whole Body of Christ worldwide?

Was Christ Surprised by the Storm in Mark 4:35–41?

Do accidents, storms, disasters, or problems that "interrupt" our callings surprise God? Did this episode in Kolkata upset his plan? Apparently not. He doesn't wring his hands in panic when we have a disaster.

Let's look at the storms in the disciples' lives for a moment.

First, there is the storm recorded in Mark 4:35–41. Their little boat was sinking, but Jesus was asleep in the bow. The poor disciples were bailing water and terrified that they might go down with the boat.

But not the Lord; the Bible says he was fast asleep in the stern. So, the disciples woke him.

"Teacher, do you not care that we are perishing?" cried the disciples in verse 36. And that's exactly how I cried out to the Lord in Kolkata.

And the Bible says that Christ awoke and rebuked the wind and said to the sea, "Peace be still!" And the wind ceased, and there was a great calm.

He said unto them, "Why are you so afraid? Have you still no faith?"

Verse 41 elaborates the problem Jesus pointed out.

"And they were filled with fear and said to one another, 'Who then is this, that even the wind and the sea obey him?'"

When you have a call from God—there is only one right way to respond to a storm. It is in faith believing, fearless obedience. Storms strengthen and exercise our faith! Storms are inevitable.

Or What about the Other Storm in Matthew 14:22–32?

Here again we see that the Lord appears to have knowingly sent his disciples into a big storm. They had rowed all night. They were afraid. But Christ was in prayer on the mountaintop. He was probably watching their struggle, and we know from other passages that he was always praying for them, just as he does for us.

The Bible says Christ "always lives to make intercession" for those who "draw near to God through him. Consequently, he is able to save to the uttermost those who draw near to God through him, since he always lives to make intercession for them" (Hebrews 7:25).

When storms come to test your calling, you may sometimes feel forsaken, but always remember that the Lord never leaves you alone in the storm.

That's how the disciples felt. They seemed to be alone and abandoned. The Bible says they were a long way from land, beaten by the waves, and "the wind was against them."

Then when they finally saw the Lord, "And in the fourth watch of the night, he came to them, walking on the sea," says Matthew 14:25. Jesus came to them again in this storm. Why? He wanted to rescue them from the stormy seas!

"They were terrified, and said 'It is a ghost!' and they cried out in fear. But immediately Jesus spoke to them, saying, 'Take heart; it is I. Do not be afraid" (verses 26-27).

He lets storms come into our lives for a good reason. John, in his inspired account of these events, says that when the Lord Jesus got into the boat, the storm ceased, and it was instantly on shore!

"And those in the boat worshiped him," says verse 33, "saying 'Truly you are the Son of God.'"

So, I learned two huge spiritual lessons in old Calcutta:

First, just because you have storms in your life doesn't mean you have missed your calling. Jesus is Lord. He is always Lord, in the good times and the bad. We must exercise faith, not fear, when test and trials come.

Second, Jesus Christ goes with us in the storms of life. Even when things go wrong by our thinking, he is there. Jesus has power over the elements. He can and does deliver us from impossible situations.

Through the Holy Spirit whom he sends to comfort us, we can have supernatural faith and see miracles too. Just like Peter, when we keep our eyes on him, we can walk on water!

When Your "Plan A" Fails, Ask God to Show You His "Plan B"

No Bible hero inspired me now as much as Paul the apostle. His missionary journeys were a source of constant inspiration to me during the Calcutta crisis. As I read about his missionary journeys, I saw how he suffered setbacks, detours, and diversions. The Holy Spirit shut and open doors, gave warnings and directions.

I was inspired by the way he landed on his feet. Paul made tents, practicing and using his vocation skills to survive. He didn't always depend on supernatural gifts, callings, and the support of Christian friends. He fully utilized his education, language skills, and the privileges of Roman citizenship as needed.

So, I began to pray in faith for Holy Spirit revelation to guide and provide. And as the Lord revealed ideas to me, I started putting them into practice. If God could sustain Paul and lead him throughout the Roman Empire, surely he could do the same for me.

Whenever I began to feel abandoned, I turned to the New Testament book of Acts. God's provision for Paul became a pattern of faith for me, and the Lord answered my cries for help.

I Praised the Lord for Past Protection and Provision

I had lost my diaries and notes during my sadhu period in Bihar, so I began to recall, recite, and write out the wonders of God's past faithfulness. I was moved by the Psalms and the Pentateuch where Moses and David recalled the victories of the Lord. As I prayer-read scriptures to the Lord, I inserted my own name and history of how the Lord had watched over me. As young as I was, I already had lots of personal examples of the Lord's intervention on my behalf.

- **The Lord had always met my needs**—I recalled God's many provisions over the years, beginning with my first Summer That Counts campaign to Spain. My childhood pastor, the Rev. Craig Massey, spontaneously collected a farewell offering just hours before I was to fly. This was unheard of at our church, the Faith Bible Church in DesPlaines, Illinois. We had strong elders, and missions' funding came from committees that had already turned me down. Calling me up to testify, he asked casually how much the mission was costing. I replied, "Seven hundred dollars." He then asked me how much I still needed to raise. I again replied, "Seven hundred dollars."

"Then, you're going totally on faith!" he shouted. "I think our church should join you in faith."

So, coming down from the pulpit, he stood me in front of the congregation, and then he asked everyone to come up and shake my hand. In each handshake, there was a five, ten, or twenty. I kept slipping the bills into my suit coat pockets. That night, the Lord supplied the $700 needed "same-day delivery." Laughing at my fears, I realized that God would provide a way out.

- **The Lord had protected me from the law and police before**—I recalled the twenty-eight times I had been detained in Franco's Spain during that Summer That Counts in 1964. La Guardia Civil, a national police force that had suppressed and persecuted Christians for decades, was harassing me as we drove from village to village in our Volkswagen van. Bible sales were legal for the first time thanks to the Vatican II Council, but this didn't stop the police from picking me up for questioning time and again. I had been stalked and followed by the police before, and the Lord delivered me. Why should I fear the Indian police now? God would deliver me out of their hands!
- **The Lord had protected me from thugs many times growing up in Chicago**—I remembered those schoolyard bullies, the teasing and the beatings I got when I was mocked as a "Protestant devil" back in Little Italy. I remembered how the Lord used the Jesuit chaplains and our local parish priest to rescue me and my brothers from my persecutors back then. Why should I fear crime here on the desperate streets of Calcutta?

I Reviewed Lives of Bible Heroes

Besides past experiences, I studied the heroes of faith in Hebrews 11. Looking back at the way the Lord had provided and protected his servants in the past gave great strength to make it through the next twenty-one days.

Waiting on God in Times of Crisis: Stranded in Kolkata

Nothing makes you pray like a crisis. There are times of trial when you need to call upon the Lord and you need to hear his guidance. It was that way now. Although Steve Isham and I were destitute and stranded in Kolkata, the Lord would make a way.

One of the most notoriously wretched cities in the world at that time, we found that we were forced to wait upon the Lord. I cannot recall if Steve was with me the whole time or exactly when he went on ahead of me to Bangkok—but he did.

However, in this time of crisis, I remember seeking the Lord and getting answers to prayer almost immediately. It was truly a day-to-day dialogue with God. You can face a crisis like this in worry or in faith. We chose faith.

We were staying in the choir loft of the William Carey Memorial Church in downtown Calcutta. It had already been leased to OM as a literature storage depot.

There, amid the dusty, worm-eaten tracts, we found a handful of cheaply printed gospels and unsold Christian books. I hit the streets and laid out the books at the commuter train stops in the downtown.

However, I quickly found the urban masses looked upon our cheaply printed propaganda with disdain. There were some expensive new Bibles in English and Bengali from the Bible Society. I laid them out on a clean, white dhoti, but there was little interest.

But there was interest in me. Lots of educated, white-collar workers stopped to talk with this white teenager from the USA. I soon realized that they were much like the Chicago office workers to whom I had sold newspapers and magazines back home.

I noticed several were carrying copies of Dale Carnegie books. He was a bestselling author in Calcutta at the time. If I only had some of those books, I knew these sharp-looking Bengalis would buy them from me.

Bookselling at Commuter Stations: *How to Win Friends and Influence People*

As I tried unsuccessfully to peddle the old Send the Light/OM books, the Lord revealed a plan to me. "Go to a book wholesaler and ask him if you can take some Dale Carnegie books out on consignment, just a handful for one morning.

"Sell those and give a free gospel of John with each book you sell," the Lord told me. "Then pay your bill in the afternoon and ask for more books to sell in the evening rush hour."

God was so specific. Who would trust me? I was only a strange, penniless white boy from Chicago. I went to find a phone book and looked up book distributors, and found that there was a warehouse within walking distance of the church.

I went to the address and found Mr. Patel chewing beetle nut and sitting there among stacks of Bengali film magazines, pornography, and English newsweeklies. He looked at me curiously.

Was this God's appointment?

I boldly asked for his help, faith, and confidence. I don't know why he trusted me or even if he fully understood my request.

He listened to me and wordlessly handed me five British paperback editions of *How to Win Friends and Influence*

People—imported copies from the UK. I knew these must be expensive books. They were sealed in cellophane to protect them from the ubiquitous dust which is everywhere in India.

Without a word, the wrapping and the way he handled those books transmitted value and cost to me.

That was the beginning of a profitable partnership with Mr. Patel. I sold them all in just one morning rush hour. Then I paid him and took five more for the evening rush. I could work out the same arrangement with the Indian Bible Society using the most expensive Bibles. Soon, I was setting up little displays of four to five self-help books, the premium Bibles, and "gospels packs" with tracts, scripture portions, and the book of John.

So, from the first day I was making enough profit to have tea and the most delicious hot chapattis for breakfast—cooked right on the street on a griddle positioned over charcoal. For the next three weeks, I was a familiar figure at the subway stop; that white boy from America with the Dale Carnegie books. Smart young men with college degrees stopped to practice their English with me. I was making friends with architects, bankers, engineers, and lawyers.

Six-story high "hoardings" at the Star Cinema loomed over Cornwallis Street (Bidhan Sarani). They offered the next James Bond movie to lines of teenage boys that never seemed to end. I was fascinated by the gigantic signage, and within minutes a Bengali teenager bought me a ticket.

That's how, by the end of the first week, I was enjoying my first James Bond film and lots of Bollywood Cinema with a new Indian friend—an older teenage boy about my age. He held my clammy hand throughout the show.

Boys holding hands with boys, and girls with girls, was quite customary in India but was still not "normal" for me.

In those twenty-one days alone in Calcutta, I had more opportunities to personally share my faith one-on-one than during the previous thirteen months.

I Fall in Love with West Bengal

I loved the Bengalis instantly—and never dreamed back in 1967 that I would return as a foreign correspondent for *Newsweek* in 1971 to watch them die by the hundreds of thousands in East Pakistan.

The War for the Liberation of Bangladesh was beyond my wildest imaginations then. Most people seemed to have little interest in politics—except for the Naxalites, a scary, far-left terrorist group of domestic Maoists.

Fanaticism—either Communist, Islamic, or Hindu—seemed far away in the City of Joy. Bigotry and hatred was something that other people did, in other places, not here in this busy place filled with young professionals.

They were far more interested in daring saris that showed bare midriffs, music, poetry, and the latest technology—wonders like transistor radios, Telex machines, and retractable ballpoint pens. Most business was still conducted with fountain pens or quills and thumb prints.

Like Johan and the brothers from Kerala on my OM team, the Bengalis had a lively curiosity about everything. They loved to speak English—even the street boys. My earlier fears of the locals were groundless. I didn't see any signs of the intense anti-Christian xenophobia that I had experienced in Rajasthan, Utter Pradesh, and Bihar. It was easy to talk about the Lord, religion, and faith; no hostility to Christ and Christianity.

Millions were living in the streets of Calcutta in the 1960's—eating, bathing, sleeping, defecating, and procreating in the open air. The smells of open-air cooking, incense, and urine competed constantly for the attention of your nostrils.

I loved it.

Old Calcutta was like Chicago. The former capital of British India was raw and full of energy and faith. I felt right at home. It was a city that thrived on transportation, trade, and knowledge. I was truly welcomed and accepted for the first time—making friends easily as one big city boy to another.

Calcutta published twenty daily newspapers in just as many languages. Plus, there were still both morning and evening editions of all the national newspapers in Bengali, Hindi, and English. Many printing presses and factories ran on steam engines that burned sugar cane and other exotic fuels.

Each morning, I was still signing in with the scowling CID officer in the local police station, but the financial pressure was off. The Lord had revealed a way for me to survive on the streets of Calcutta.

My faith was growing, and I eagerly horded each rupee for my air ticket. By faith, I booked a ticket on the appointed deadline departure date for Rangoon. I was allowed to break my journey there but was required to buy an "open ticket" onto Bangkok. Return to India was forbidden.

I think the one-way ticket was only eighty-eight dollars, but that was like $1,000 to me. By the grace of God, I had sold just enough books to buy the ticket on the very day before I left. My earnings could not have been more than twenty-five cents from each sale. That ticket alone was a miracle.

The Lord knows the way through the wilderness, I sang, *all I have to do is to follow!*

The next morning, I turned myself in at the police station and was taken into custody again. They drove me to the airport in an Ambassador squad car. There I was escorted to the plane.

The same unsmiling immigration officer that had first arrested me was planeside holding up my passport.

Before he turned it over to me, he lectured me again.

"Your visa is void," he repeated. "You are blacklisted and are not welcome in India. Any attempt to return would make you subject to arrest and imprisonment."

His words hit me like a death sentence. I could not reconcile them with my call to Rajasthan. I knew that God was still my shield, defender and lifter up of my head. *If he wanted me back in India, he would make it happen,* I tried to assure myself with all the faith I could work up.

And he did! I was chastised but ended up coming back to India many times in the decades that followed. When I returned to India, it was often as an honored guest of my Indian media friends and the Foreign Ministry. I frequently came on journalist visa and was once even embedded with the Indian Army. Another time I was honored with a doctorate degree from the Emmanuel Seminary in Kota.

Burma on My Mind

At that moment, however, returning to India was the last thing on my mind! God was indeed closing the door and I had come to accept it as his will.

For the first time, I felt that God was really leading me to leave. Somehow, I knew I was safely in his hands. I didn't know how, but in my heart I knew he was overruling in this forced exit.

Like William Carey in Calcutta, Adnoniram Judson and his pioneer work in Burma was also a romantic inspiration to me. Burma was an attractive destination to me. I had Burma on my mind, and I looked forward to stopping there—of walking the streets Judson had walked.

I even believed that I would be able to stay in Burma, perhaps indefinitely. Maybe I could start all over. The guidebooks said they gave Americans fifteen-day tourist visas at the border. I dreamed that I could get one and work from there.

How wrong I was.

In Burma, I didn't get past immigration desk!

I soon found myself in another police lock-up. One look at my Indian *persona non-grata* was enough for these stern guards. There was no need to check with higher officials. The brutal military government then in power didn't want penniless hippies or "Jesus people" in Burma. If the Indians didn't want me, then neither did they—even as a tourist.

Burmese immigration informed me to take a seat and wait. They had called the American Embassy and someone was coming to talk with me. I saw a pattern developing. It was like Calcutta all over again.

Meanwhile the plane took off without me.

Shortly, another athletic, very American-looking Ivy Leaguer showed up—or was it the same strong man I had met back in India? There was something authoritative, scary, and powerful about his trim, militarized body.

He seemed just like the overly-trained assistant I had met in Calcutta at the Immigration Office there.

"That's it," I realized. "This guy is some kind of soldier on a mission."

He seemed to know me already. He obviously had no time for small talk. He was all business and didn't even bother to introduce himself. He casually picked up the conversation "where we had left off" in Calcutta.

I was Bangkok Bound

Again, he pressed a Ricardo Negro State Department business card into my hand—commanding me to take a taxi to the Consulate on Wireless Road in Bangkok.

"You will only have a seventy-two-hour transit visa in Thailand. You must see Ricardo Negro right away—so go straight to the embassy on *Soi Whittaya*. Be there when the consulate opens.

"He's expecting you and he'll get you a Thai visa," he said, deliberately ignoring my puzzled look.

How could the Americans get me a Thai visa? I wondered.

"Don't worry," he said as he continued to read my face, "Negro has connections." As a Chicago boy, I understood connections.

So, that's how my first mission to what had formerly been British India came to a bittersweet end. There, in that sweltering Rangoon holding area, I admitted defeat.

God had mysteriously closed the door to modern India. I was Bangkok bound for sure, like it or not.

Later that night, I was escorted onto a Pan Am flight to Bangkok. As we walked up the boarding stairs, my passport was returned to me. Again, with an offensive red stamp that meant it could never be used legally again in Burma.

I was too young in my walk with God to understand it all—but there on that plane I again felt the strong, loving presence of the Lord. I gave God the only thing I had left, my total trust and obedience. And it was enough. The heavens were satisfied, and I was filled with his glory as the plane took off for Thailand.

Only later would I understand it all. God uses you—but mostly in the times when you don't even know it!

Below me in the moonlight was mile after mile of rice paddy.

I landed after midnight and spent the dawn hours trying to sleep in the lobby of the Don Maung International Airport.

Demon voices returned to taunt me for a time; I was forgotten and forsaken, they said. My time in India had been a failure, they repeated—and would repeat for years to come. Satan doesn't easily give up on a good lie when he finds it is working to depress your soul.

I was discouraged. It seemed—at least from a human viewpoint—that I had gone on a fool's errand. *Maybe,* I thought in self-pity, *all my critics at home and in India where right after all.*

This whole mission seemed ill-conceived, poorly executed, unappreciated, and unwanted. It wasn't hard to for me to be humble at that moment. I had nothing to brag about. I was sure not the "missionary hero" I thought I would be—the next Judson or Carey or Hudson Taylor.

So, I had to trust the Lord—and it was not quite as easy to do as I batted at mosquitos that night.

Soon I got over it as I praised and thanked the Lord out of habit. God had miraculously delivered me. Angels seemed to be protecting me. I was not alone.

Praise the Lord, I repeated to myself over and over in the warm, clean air.

One of the blessings of human failure is the closeness it brings you with the Lord. The Holy Spirit comforted me. My mission was accomplished although I didn't understand it. I had obeyed the Lord. I could cry out to Jesus in the words of Job, "Though he slay me, I will hope in him" (Job 13:15).

And something had happened. I had learned the secrets of submission—I had learned the essentials of living a yielded life. I had walked through all five of the waypoints to a yielded life. In the final chapter, we will examine them one by one. It is the most important and useful chapter in this book. Don't put this book down yet.

Chapter 7

Five Waypoints to a Yielded Life

Trust in the Lord with all your heart, and do not lean on your own understanding. In all your ways acknowledge him, and he will make straight your paths.
—Proverbs 3:5–6

I promised you this moment when we began our journey together. Way back in the introduction, I said that we would arrive at this point. Here is the moment of revelation—the simple roadmap to living a yielded life.

So, please get ready to absorb the "take home" from my story. Find a quiet corner somewhere to read the rest in sacred solitude—preferably in a silent place where you won't be disturbed. (I personally find the best such spaces early in the morning while the rest of the world is still sleeping!)

You can count the five waypoints on one hand. And here they are, just as I discovered them through the events in this book:

(1) Say Yes to God: *Pray Always*

(2) Know His Will: *Do the Word of God*
(3) Choose to Believe: *Practice Faith*
(4) Unite with His Body: *Work in Harmony*
(5) Yield to His Spirit: *Overcome the Flesh*

These are the five mighty battering rams that will knock down the gates of hell in your life. You can live this life. Jesus is calling you. Say yes today to the call of God.

Nothing can stop you if you do. Yield this minute and the barrier that seems so large to you will collapse. This is what Jesus promised—the barriers that Satan erects will not stand against you. We are the sheep of his pasture and our Good Shepherd will make a way for us. God has equipped us with all we need to break every chain.

That includes chains of indifference, ignorance, unbelief, disunity, and powerlessness. All you need is the constant practice of prayer, obedience to the Word of God, using faith believing to implement the Word, gathering with the church, and the baptism of Holy Spirit.

In this way, no weapon formed against you will prosper. You have all you need to navigate through every danger. There is dynamite in the power that raised Christ from the dead—dynamite in my life and yours as we practice these five disciplines.

You too have a "Kota Junction" call in your life, something God has for you like he had for me when he called to Rajasthan. Reaching it will lead you past and through these five waypoints:

Waypoint 1—Say Yes to God in Prayer. Everything begins with prayer. Learn to truly pray, to dialogue with God continuously. Keep seeking God and you will find him. Real prayer is not coming to God with a list of your wants and needs. It is actively listening to God and taking the next step he shows you, wherever it leads.

I came to that first waypoint when God appeared to me that night in Crowell Hall. I sought him in prayer, and he came to me. I did not find him. He found me! It was all his doing, not mine. It was grace awakening in my life.

It wasn't that I had earned his special favor. Nothing like that. I was not fasting, confessing sins, earning merit, seeking holiness, practicing flagellation, doing good works of righteousness and self-sacrifice! I had simply gotten into the habit of saying yes to God—and that night I was saying yes again.

I am not writing against good works and spiritual disciplines, but while practicing piety, we need to remember the glorious promise of grace in James 4:8, "Draw near to God, and he will draw near to you ..."

I am not saying "drawing near to God" is something we do without personal cost. The promise in James 4:8 is made in the context of a strict warning against pride and worldliness. Drawing near to God is not always easy.

When the Lord visited me that night at Moody Bible Institute, he was simply drawing near to me in response to my willingness to seek his face for India. I had just said yes to God on a matter that was close to his heart. I was agreeing with him. This is ultimate prayer—the highest point in our devotion to him.

He was delighted in me because I was delighted in him! He was giving me the delight of my heart because my heart was focused on him! India was on the heart of the Lord so suddenly; it was on mine too!

Prayer is syncing your will with God's will. He wants the voluntary surrender of your heart and mind to his.

Jesus says, "And I tell you, ask, it will be given to you; seek, and you will find; knock, and it will be opened to you. For every one who asks receives, and the one who seeks finds, and to one who knocks, it will be opened" (Luke 11:9–10).

This passage, from Christ's teaching to the disciples on prayer, is to me like the thumb of my right hand. The thumb is the most important finger because you can't get a grip anything without your thumb.

Jesus was talking in Luke 11:1–13 within the context of receiving Holy Spirit from the Father through prayer (see verse 13).

With that baptism of Holy Spirit comes the guidance you so desperately want; the Spirit comes alongside us as a comforter to show us the way.

This kind of biblical prayer involves many stages. My friend and mentor Dick Eastman spells it out by creating an acronym with the word ACTS. It is short for (1) adoration, (2) confession, (3) thanksgiving, and (4) supplication.

This is the kind of prayer we see practiced by the prophet in Daniel 9:1–19. It incorporated confession, supplication, and thanksgiving with adoration.

ADORATION: We see that this kind of adoration includes waiting on God and listening for the things that delight his heart. It is impossible to do listening prayer without waiting on God. Waiting on the Lord is a fundamental prayer discipline that is basic to everything else in your relationship to him.

The scriptures reveal much about God to adore—especially in the Psalms. I have found that praying the psalms out loud is a wonderful way to enter his presence. And as you adore him by praying the Psalms, you will find every emotional and psychological need you have will be met. Pray them daily for the rest of your life. Get to know them intimately and every pain in your heart will be healed.

CONFESSION: Scripture also helps us to identify and confess our sins, thank God for his graces, and make supplications so that his will is done on earth as it is heaven. Both in the Lord's Prayer found in Matthew 6 and in Daniel's model prayer, we see a kind of order.

THANKSGIVING: We enter his gates with thanksgiving and praise in our hearts. We don't begin our time of prayer by asking for things!

Too much of what we commonly call prayer is focused on verbally addressing requests to God. As children, and even as young believers, I think we are taught too soon to ask God for things.

This is a Hollywood portrayal of the Lord. It panders to our natural human tendencies. We usually don't go to God unless we are sick or needy or have a problem. He is too often portrayed as a celestial Santa Claus—the one we go to only when something is too big for us to handle in our own strength.

Many religious leaders, even those of pagan, non-Christian denominations, teach this distorted, one-sided approach to prayer. Religious charlatans and soothsayers often have it in their bag of tricks.

Thus, it is easy to forget that real prayer begins when you shut up and listen. Prayer is not primarily talking to God; it is listening, waiting, seeking, and knocking. It begins with a heart-attitude of submission—waiting upon God to know his heart and obey his will for you.

SUPPLICATION: Out of our waiting comes knowledge of the Lord and what he wants to accomplish in our lives and in the situations around us. That's when real intercession can begin. God longs to hear our petitions when they are aligned with his will and way.

We fail to realize that nothing is outside the power of prayer except that which is outside the will of God.

Prayer is like the thumb on your right hand. Everything starts with it, and it is the finger that holds everything else together.

But how can we pray in faith believing if we don't know what to pray for ... if we have not found his will? How do we know for sure that we are praying rightly? This question leads us to Waypoint 2.

Waypoint 2—Know His Will. The Bible commands us to know the will of God, "Therefore do not be foolish, but understand what the will of the Lord is" (Ephesians 5:17). We are required to know his will. How can we do that? By considering the Word of God every day. It is that easy.

Most people struggle with finding the will of God because they really don't want to do it! I know that's still true for me—it's only hard when my mind is already made up on something. Instead of conforming my will to prayers to his calling, I am trying to force God to do my will.

So, do you want to be sure of your calling?

Then begin each day in the Word of God! Before you make any decision, know what the Lord has revealed about it in his written word. Study to be approved. Remember, 99.9 percent of the will of God is already recorded for us in the Bible.

The Word of God Is the Will of God

Once I said yes to God's call on my life, it was amazing how quickly everything began to fall right in place. Back at Moody in '64, for example, I found all the answers to the big questions in my life resolved in less than two semesters—academic majors, career choices, dating and sex, a marriage partner, vocations, and even what to do on spring break.

The so called "big questions" were no longer as large when I started believing and obeying what the Word of God said on these issues in my life.

Anytime I wasn't sure, all I usually had to do was go to 1 Corinthians 13, Ephesians 4–5, Philippians 3, Colossians 3–4, or Galatians 5–6.

There is no real mystery about this. The Word is "God breathed" and comes from above. He has spoken out his will. God has clearly made it known to us in black and white.

"All scripture is breathed out by God and profitable for teaching, for reproof, for correction and for training in righteousness that the man of God may be competent, equipped for every good work" (2 Timothy 3:16–17).

- The Word of God gives us what to teach; doctrine is defined as right believing—and it is profitable for "doctrine," says the King James Version.
- It reproves us at points where we are not living righteously.
- It corrects us when we go off track into disobedience or sin, shows us how to get back to right believing.
- It trains us in righteousness.
- But that doesn't mean we become sinless. In fact, the daily disciplines of reflection, contrition, and confession become a way of life for us as we faithfully reflect our actions against the revealed will of God in the Bible. "If we confess our sins, he is faithful and just to forgive us our sins and cleanse us from all unrighteousness" (1 John 1:9).

The Word of God assures us that we can be crowned as overcomers, victors, and winners in the game of life. We all have obstacles to overcome—secret spiritual alliances with the world, the flesh, and the devil. My biggest obstacles, it seemed to me at the time, were in my flesh.

The Word of God pointed the way out for me.

"How shall a young man cleanse his way?" asks the psalmist.

"By taking heed to the word," comes the answer.

Ever since, I think of the Word of God as my pointer finger. It guides the way to holy, separated living.

When you accept the call of God on your life, you are consecrated and set apart to accomplish a task. How do you know what it is and how to do it?

You begin praying for God's will to be done on earth as it is above. How will you know what that will is? The Bible tells you so.

Just a final warning about relying on emotions, experiences, revelations, and leadings. These "feelings" and "hunches" must conform to the written word of God.

Called to All

When they don't, God will intervene. Sometimes, very dramatically. He has his ways of getting our attention. In Acts 9:15, we see that God called Paul to be a "chosen vessel" in a blinding light. And he uses circumstances, sickness and death if has too.

Does that mean everyone must be struck down by a blinding light? Of course not! That seems to be almost unique to Paul. Must you have a vision? Dream? An epiphany, fleece, revelation, feeling, or hear an audible voice?

No. Not at all. God doesn't work that way with most normal people! Only the self-centered, proud and stubborn seem to need such signs. And even then, no sign is given without confirmation, usually multiple confirmations. Never is a sign given in contradiction to the revealed will of God in scripture.

Knowing the will of God leads us to Waypoint 3.

Waypoint 3—Choose to Believe and Do It. It isn't enough to just know the truth; you must believe it. Faith without works is dead.

"And without faith," says the Bible, "it is impossible to please him, for whoever would draw near to God must believe that he exists and the he rewards those who seek him." (Hebrews 11:6).

Faith is an action verb in the Bible, not a noun. That's true not just here in Hebrews 11:6 but everywhere in the New Testament.

It should be translated and read, "And without *believing*, it is impossible to please him ..."

When we launched out in obedience to the vision of our call, finances began to manifest. I no longer had my newsstand business to sustain me—but the Lord supplied for our Christmas campaign in Monterrey, Mexico, and again on our spring break in Canada and again on Chicago's South Side for the Summer in the City. We were destitute. Yet money manifested itself in our lives and ministries.

I cannot remember a time when we didn't have what we needed. Our needs were met because we were believing they would be met per the promises of God's word.

By the time it came to leave for Europe and regions beyond, the funds were in the bank, at least for the airfare and approved budget! We believed that God had called and that he would supply—and he did.

One of the saddest passages in the life of Christ is recorded in Matthew 13:53–58. Jesus returned home to Nazareth after healing and casting out demons in Galilee, but the Bible says, "He did not do many mighty works there because of their unbelief." In Mark 6:6, it says that Jesus "marveled" at their unbelief. Some versions say he was "amazed" at their unbelief.

By way of explanation, Jesus said to them, "A prophet is not without honor, except in his hometown and among his relatives and in his own household." These people heard his teachings and knew his word but chose not to believe. They were overly familiar with Jesus. They despised and underestimated him.

So, it is possible for us who know the scriptures to still disbelieve them—to have contempt for the written promises of God, the ones which he has made to those who believe. This is calling God a liar.

There are hundreds of verses on this theme in the New Testament. Everything in God's economy hinges on faith believing, including the New Testament plan of salvation. "For by grace you have been saved through faith" (Ephesians 2:8-9) and Romans 10:9-10, "because if you confess with your mouth that Jesus is Lord and believe in your heart that God raised him from the dead, you will be saved. For with the heart one believes and is justified ..."

Faith, like love, is an action word, a verb. Not to practice "believing" is to commit the sin of unbelieving. Not to love is the same as committing the sin of hating and murder in Christ's spiritual economy.

How often do we repent of unbelief, of doubting God?

No surprise then that my "big middle finger" reminds me of faith. It is the strongest finger of all. But the finger of faith, to work, must be united with the others. That brings us to Waypoint 4.

Waypoint 4—Unite with the Body of Christ. Don't try to walk this road alone. Do it with the church, with other called-out ones. It's a team effort. The Lord is looking for harmony.

In John 15, Jesus says he is the vine and we are the branches. Only as we abide in him, he warns, will we bear much fruit. So, everything starts out of our union with Christ and his body, out of his love, and within his body.

Everything is God in Christ ... Christ in you ... and you in the Body of Christ. This is a mind-boggling truth.

This is the secret of entering your work and calling. It makes our prayer life amazing. It is the secret of entering the presence of God in prayer. So, it guides our approach to the Father.

The only way we can be seated on the throne next to Father is to be "in Christ." Christ is right now seated on the right hand of the Father where he "is interceding for us" per Romans 8:34. You can't get any closer to God than to be in Christ and in his body.

And how do we know the mind of Christ? Through practicing the Word of God with the people of God. In Christ alone we can say, "Our Father in heaven, hollowed be your name. Your kingdom come, your will be done, on earth as it is heaven" (Matthew 6:10).

Rarely in the New Testament are the promises or petitions of God given in the singular. It is telling that this petition from the so-called Lord's Prayer is addressed to "our Father" not "my Father."

Everything is interconnected. We are the Body of Christ. He has no hands but our hands. He has no feet but our feet. We are left here as his manifest presence on this earth.

When God called me, it is significant that I was not called alone. I was chosen for his service from out of a group. We were a missionary prayer circle—a group of mostly single women praying for God's will to be done in India as it is in heaven. We men were a distinct minority, but without the women we would not have been sent.

Rosemary Turner and her women united with me in faith-believing prayer. And beyond that, they supported me on my mission—and others like them still do today. I am not a lone ranger. United prayer creates united action—results. Prayer is action.

Sure, I faced hatred, opposition, and persecution in obeying my call after that night, but I faced those trials because Lew Williams, Steve Isham, George, and scores of others supported me with their faith, intercession, sacrifice, and offerings.

Only much later, did I find that people unknown to me around the world on every continent were praying for a Rajasthan Gospel Team or the North India Boys Team. I was not alone. We were not alone. We did not go out alone any more that the Apostle Paul went out alone.

Most of all, Christ was with us. Jesus said, "Where two or three are gathered in my name, there am I among them" (from Matthew 18:20).

Note that our Lord made this promise in the context of teaching on prayer. United prayer has the power to bring the presence of God into a situation. "Truly, I say to you, whatever you bind on earth shall be bound in heaven, and whatever you lose on earth shall be loosed in heaven. Again, I say to you, if any two of you agree on earth about anything they ask, it shall be done unto them" (Matthew 18:18–19).

Beware of taking any action on your own! Unity is where God commands life per Psalm 133:3, "For there the Lord has commanded the blessing, life forever." United faith. United action. United prayer is precious to God. "Behold how good and how pleasant it is when brothers to dwell in unity" (Psalm 133:1).

Thank God, we are not left alone to figure out the will of God. Not only is the God-breathed Word written down for us by the prophets, we have another one to illuminate it for us—the Holy Spirit.

And this scripture-revealed Word from God is of no private interpretation. As we study it daily and in context of every situation, we can easily adjust our flight path and make corrections.

If you are going to avoid private interpretation in discerning the meaning of scriptures, it means that group Bible study is going to be a team effort too!

The only cure when we get off track is daily repentance. That is prompted from constant study, prayer, and obedient action. Line up everything you do with the Word of God, live a life of prayer, and start each day waiting upon God for instructions, and then work as a team—always reporting to a trusted accountability group!

The phrase "correct me if I'm wrong" should roll easily off our tongues as we fulfill our callings in small groups.

United Prayer, Study and Action

Study. Prayer. Action. That's the ideal definition of how a good small group should be organized. This is real unity. It combines Waypoints 1–4 on the path to the yielded life. I started several accountability growth groups at MBI, and throughout my life I have constantly sought the comfort and guidance of united prayer groups.

I call these SPA Groups or SPA Clubs (short for study, prayer, and action). You can organize a SPA club as a couple, a trio, or quartet—or have all three going at once!

At any rate, I was far from conforming my life to the scriptures when I started out on this journey. Besides my struggle with pride, I was keeping and feeding "pet sins." I lived in denial, refusing to acknowledge them—convinced that I could somehow manage and keep them under control, refusing to recognize them for what they were.

These secret realms of self-will were idols that had to go—and go they did as I yielded to the Holy Spirit and the Lord began to do his promised work in me. "But I say, walk by the Spirit and you not gratify the desires of the flesh" (Galatians 5:16).

Unless you deal with them, they will become lifelong struggles, unless you form accountability growth groups as a way of life.

My ring finger reminds me of this Waypoint 4. It is where the wedding band goes in most Western cultures. It represents fidelity and faithfulness—and not just to my marriage partner but to all my friends in the larger Body of Christ.

Teamwork is the key. "For the whole law is fulfilled in one word: You shall love your neighbor as yourself. But if you devour one another, watch out that you are consumed by one another" (Galatians 5:14–15).

So, don't try to live a yielded life alone. The yielded life is never done solo. Which leads us to the greatest secret of all, uniting our efforts with the will of God through his Spirit. That's Waypoint 5.

Waypoint 5—Yielding to the Holy Spirit. This is the final and most amazing secret of living a yielded life: *The power to follow your calling comes not from within yourself but from an external source!*

"Know ye not," writes Paul under the inspiration of the Holy Spirit, "that to whom ye yield yourselves servants to obey, his servants ye are to whom ye obey; whether of sin unto death, or of obedience unto righteousness?" (Romans 6:16, KJV).

When you yield to the Holy Spirit, power from on high comes flowing through your body and mind with the force of a mighty, rushing wind! That's dynamic, gale-force winds! There's power. Resurrection power. Death to life power.

This happened to me, just as it did to Peter when he preached his Pentecost sermon to the collected Judeans and converts from all over the world.

Called to All

The Holy Spirit manifests power. Supernatural power. Others see it. God has promised it—as a sign especially to unbelievers.

For me, I began to manifest this power during our 1965 Summer in the City Campaign on Chicago's Southside. We were distributing tracts and witnessing at the Forty-Third Street CTA stop on the Southbound Red Line when I glanced at the magazine display. I was shocked and then spiritually enraged by some of the vile pornography on display.

Without a second thought, the Lord led me to pick up some samples of the material and I led our whole tract team on a loop-bound train to the Merchandise Mart—to the offices of the Chicago Transit Authority. From my years in the newsstand business, I knew where to go.

Handing out tracts as we rode along, I led the team to the CTA offices that dealt with concessions and newsstands. I ran a newsstand for years, so I was sure that these publications were banned.

I was so furious in the Holy Spirit that I led the whole team in a protest right in the very offices where pornography was banned, controlled and permitted. The police were called while I waited to see the transit authorities. They made the team go downstairs to the lobby where they continued to witness while I remained upstairs. They allowed me to stay and officially voice our complaint.

Manifesting the Gift of Prophecy

I unfolded the magazines to display the nudity and perversion to the staff in charge, denouncing the pornography with supernatural force and power.

I was anointed. Empowered. Filled with the Spirit.

The women in the room blushed furiously at the sight of the pictures. They agreed fully with my denunciations of this literature. Who could stand against my charges? My words had convicting power. The gross images in these poses showed victims of ungodly abuse, brutality, and humiliation.

Even the police agreed. I was winning the case as I prophesied in the power of the Lord. Conviction from the Holy Spirit overcame my nominally Catholic hearers. They were not necessarily born-again Christians. Yet they promised a crackdown on the CTA newsstands that were selling the smut—and on the distributor responsible.

Then, as I was successfully making the case against the porn, I realized that something incredibly holy and supernatural had come over me. What was I saying? What was coming out of my mouth? Where had this power and courage come from? I realized that I was manifesting the gift of prophecy—the power of God.

What a contrast to the old Billy Bray.

There was a time, only a year or two earlier, when I would have self-righteously argued against all anti-obscenity laws. I had made an absolute 180-degree turn. When I owned a news business, I wanted all such bans lifted.

Now, here I was holding back the seventies sexual revolution which was already creeping across the city. I was also holding back the judgement of God on the City of Chicago.

This literature was still illegal at the time but available everywhere for "under-the-counter sale." In other words, you couldn't legally sell it, but the police looked the other way if you didn't display it openly.

In fact, just a couple years earlier, I considered pornography a sophisticated joke. I believed in the *Playboy* philosophy and read Hugh Hefner's columns regularly. Not only that, I was sexually curious and addicted.

What had happened to me that summer of '65? Why the change?

Yielding Makes All the Difference

What happened? I was yielding to the Holy Spirit in my life, that's what! That summer, I began to consciously and deliberately yield. I was already a born-again believer. I had possession of Holy Spirit power from on high—but like so many believers, I was holding out on Jesus Christ.

This is why the church appears weak, unfruitful and powerless.

I had the Holy Spirit in my heart and life, but I chose not to use it.

Before that, I was insubordinate to my Lord. Proud. Stubborn. Self-willed.

Can that happen? You bet it can. "Carnal Christians" go by many names, but sadly it is the way that most Christians relate to the Lord most of the time!

Now, that had changed. I had been filled with the Spirit. Suddenly, I no longer looked at erotica the way I used to view it. The way I used to live was no longer acceptable to me. I was amazed at the change.

Regarding pornography, for example, I had changed my tune. Now I was reacting with indignation because the pure Spirit of the Lord was enjoying full reign in my life.

Jesus said, "But you will receive power when the Holy Spirit has come upon you, and you will be my witnesses in Jerusalem and in all Judea and Samaria, and to the end of the earth" (Acts 1:8).

Power to witness. That's what the Holy Spirit gives us when we yield.

God wants us all to be baptized in the Holy Spirit and living it out.

That summer, I began to manifest all the other gifts of the Holy Spirit as listed in First Corinthians 12:4–7: "Now there are varieties of gifts, but the same Spirit; and there are varieties of service, but the same Lord; and there are varieties of activities but it is the same God who empowers them all in everyone. To each is given the manifestation of the Sprit for the common good."

That summer, I began to hate the world, the flesh, and devil. I fell in love with Jesus. I was filled with the Spirit as the Bible demands, and I began to manifest the baptism of the Holy Spirit. That's the normal Christian life.

My Little Finger Is a Daily Reminder to Me!

My little finger is the final finger reminder on my hand—the reminder that I need to yield to the Holy Spirit! It is small and often goes unnoticed, but like the thumb, it is essential for getting a good grip on anything. It is the last and the least but essential to fully using your spiritual hand. Together with the thumb, it helps you get a grip on any challenge in your life.

This Holy Spirit power is not for an elite few. It is promised to every believer. You can let the power of God control your life if you will only yield. When you do, you will find yourself naturally manifesting the power as needed in every situation.

If you are a born-again believer, you have the Holy Spirit. If you are not manifesting it in your life, *you just need to start yielding.* (However, if not, it probably means that you are not a born-again believer!)

If you are not yet born-again—if you are still holding out—then you need to obey Romans 10:9–10. I repeat it again, "If you confess with your mouth that Jesus is Lord and believe in your heart that God raised him from the dead, you will be saved. For with the heart one believes and is justified, and with the mouth one confesses and is saved."

On the day of Pentecost, Peter said to them in Acts 2:38, "Repent, and let every one of you be baptized in the name of Jesus Christ for the remission of sins; and you shall receive the gift of the Holy Spirit."

Have you ever consciously yielded your will to the Holy Spirit? Do you feel that you might still be playing a tug-of-war with God over this matter? Are you tired of yielding to your flesh and ready to start yielding to the Spirit?

Is Today the Time for You to Surrender?

Then why not hoist the white flag on the castle of your heart today? Surrender yourself to the Lord. Yield to the Holy Spirit.

Although I am not advocating "tarrying" meetings and the emotionalism long associated with them here in the United States, I realize that due to the mysteries involved in such surrender, this may take some time in your life.

It is not so much chronological time but spiritual time that is required—what the Bible calls kairos. We must reach the time where we are ready to surrender.

Even though I was raised in a God-fearing, religious home, I resisted the Holy Spirit's leading for years. It is possible for Christians to become self-dependent and full of pride. I was. That's an important part of my story. My calling. And it could very well be a part of your search to obey the call of God on your life.

I had to finally come to the end of myself and sincerely yield to the Holy Spirit. I did this alone one night in the predawn hours in my mom's Jefferson Park living room. At that moment, the Lord manifested the Holy Spirit with power from on high. If you're at that place now as you read my words, I want to encourage you to open your heart to the Lord.

Jesus promised to send us the Holy Spirit, a comforter who would lead us into all truth, "If you love me, you will keep my commandments. And I will ask the Father, and he will give you another Helper, to be with you forever, even the Spirit of Truth, whom the world cannot receive, because it neither sees him nor knows him. You know him, for he dwells with you and will be in you ... I will not leave you as orphans ... Whoever does not love me does not keep my words. And the word that you hear is not mine, but the Father's who sent me ... the Helper, the Holy Spirit, whom the Father will send in my name, he will teach you all things and bring to your remembrance all that I have said to you ..." (John 14:15-26).

Do not struggle another day to fulfill your call without the power of the Holy Spirit. If these words are for you, give up your carnal ways now. Stop trying to live out your calling in the power of the flesh. Join me in living in the spiritual power of a yielded life.

I challenge you to walk intentionally through these five spiritual waypoints—not just now as you read them—but every day. They are biblical disciplines, all interlocking and feeding into each other.

Then, let me know how things are going in your life. Follow these biblical principles in league with others, and I believe that you will suddenly be propelled forward into fulfilling your mission for God.

You have a calling. I can't exactly tell you what it is. But I know there is a God-ordained mission for every man, woman, boy, and girl in this world. God has put you here for a purpose, and following these five waypoints will help you find it afresh each day. Finding the will of God is an ongoing process—not a one-time event.

It is a life-long journey. There will probably be multiple calls and callings as time goes by. In each stage of your life, you will have new opportunities to faithfully yield your way through to the next episode.

Will you listen for and obey your calling? God is still calling as he did in Isaiah 6:8. Will you answer as Isaiah did when he heard the call?

He wrote under the power of the Holy Spirit, "And I heard the voice of the Lord saying, "Whom shall I send, and who will go for us?"

Then I said, "Here am I! Send me."

Epilogue

George went on from those early Send the Light days to become known to millions around the world as George Verwer, the founder of Operation Mobilization (OM). At the time of our North Indian blitzes, OM was an exploding outreach of Send the Light.

He served for forty-six years as international director of STL/OM. Today, after sixty years, OM is one of the leading mission agencies in the world with 6,800 staff and volunteers serving the Lord in 118 countries. Through the years, OM ships like the *Logos/Hope* have plied the seven seas hosting book and media fairs.

George is author of eight books, including his latest from Moody Press, *Messiology—The mystery of how God works even when it doesn't make sense to us.* Over one hundred ministries and international organizations have grown out of OM, including the Christian Information Service, Inc., which was first organized by Billy Bray as the Thailand Christian Information Service during his Bangkok years.

George yielded his life to Christ in the 1955 Billy Graham, New York crusade when he was a young businessman. A lifelong lover of books and media, his impact on Billy Bray was pivotal. He challenged Billy Bray to seek and find God's calling on his life and was his first cross-cultural missions mentor. With his wife, Drena, George lived for a time with Billy in Bangkok during his Thailand mission from 1967-1973.

Johan went on to become K.P. Yohannan, founder of Gospel for Asia, India's largest indigenous mission agency and a bishop in The Believers Church. Author of *Revolution in World Missions*, Yohannan yielded his life to God on an OM outreach. From there, the Lord used him to build and influence a global network of mission leaders. He has helped raise billions of dollars for the indigenous missions' movement.

Gospel for Asia (GFA) now minsters among thousands of unreached people groups in twelve countries. He has a global support team for Indian outreach with followers on every continent.

For more than thirty years, Gospel for Asia has provided humanitarian assistance and spiritual hope to millions across Asia, especially among those who have yet to hear the Good News. In 2015, this included more than 75,000 sponsored children, free medical services for more than 180,000 people, 6,000 wells drilled, 11,000 water filters installed, Christmas presents for more than 400,000 needy families, and spiritual teaching available in 110 languages in fourteen nations through radio ministry.

Yohannan has authored, edited or published two hundred revolutionary books, including nine titles in America. His weekly radio broadcast, *Road to Reality*, is heard on eight hundred US radio stations. *The Coming Revolution in World Missions, Road to Reality, Why the World Waits,* and *Touching Godliness* are his most popular titles dealing with the call of God in English.

Billy Bray went on to spend the next fifty years as an author, bi-vocation media missionary, mentor, teacher, and journalist. Through it all, he has sought to be a servant to Christ, world evangelism, and hundreds of post-colonial indigenous missions' movements.

He founded the Christian Information Service (CIS, Inc.). As a media missionary, William Thomas Bray focused on developing indigenous missions and charitable movements to "Finish the Task" on every continent. He has trained over three hundred indigenous leaders in missions' development and communications from his Virginia base—mostly with Christian Aid and Overseas Students Mission.

As an author and journalist, writing under various bylines, he relentlessly struggled to find and expose the truth in both the church and the world, providing news to hundreds of publications and broadcasts.

He worked on staff or as a freelancer with ABC News, Assist News, the *Bangkok Post*, the *Bangkok World*, *Christian Aid* magazine, *Christian Life* magazine, CIS News, the *Lane Daily*, *Newsweek* magazine, Reuters, the *Wheaton Journal*, and *World Vision* magazine. He has done thousands of freelance assignments. Since he retired in 2013 from Christian Aid Mission, he has continued to write and serve international students and overseas visitors as chairman of the Overseas Students Mission.

Called to All: How I Discovered the Power of a Yielded Life is the thirteenth mission book on which he has collaborated, either anonymously or under his own byline.

The Rest of the Story

The Lord opened amazing doors of opportunity for Bray during those early years in Bangkok. He became a bi-vocational Christian feature writer and editor—a kind of "Journalist for Jesus" in and to the mass media.

Over the years, he fought battles with depression, guilt and regret over his early mission to India. The apparent failure of the 1966 Rajasthan Blitz became a shameful memory he sought to hide for years.

Then, during the decades that followed, came an amazing revelation.

His faithful man, K. P. Yohannan, who he had left behind in India become the North Indian field director for Operation Mobilization. After a time as an international student in

Singapore and Dallas, he cashed in a life insurance policy and started the indigenous mission that became Gospel for Asia.

Again, he linked up with Billy Bray who consulted and worked with him as an adviser, editor and writer in Wheaton, Illinois. Finally, he joined the full-time staff at GFA headquarters in Carrollton, Texas.

Year by year that commitment grew. As the decades passed, the work spread to every state in India and many surrounding countries. K.P.'s early books became best sellers, and he became a global spokesman for indigenous-led missions. Support offices were started in Australia, Europe, and around the world.

That little operation has grown to 23,000 missionaries, thousands of churches, and over fifty Bible schools.

Suddenly it all made sense to Bray!

God had sent him to India, not to become a successful missionary as he fancied, but to help disciple a man who would. God had called him to throw away plans for his personal career, education, fiancée, family heritage, and reputation.

Like John the Baptist, he realized that God had called him to decrease in order that another might increase.

"Many never live long enough to see the fruit of such obedience to God's call," says Bray, "It is a joy just to see fruit that remains. But the called one doesn't—or shouldn't—care about such things.

"He or she is working for the Lord, and leaves the results with God. You yield, and that's enough.

"In my case, because I obeyed my first call as a teenager, I can look back and see fourth and fifth generations of indigenous missionaries finishing the task today. In once-dead places like Rajasthan—today, there is a living, growing church.

"I hope and pray that my story will encourage others to obey their calls and leave the results to the Lord. That's why I wrote *Called to All*."

Jesus is Lord Even When It Doesn't Make Sense to Us

God has everything under control. History shows that despite all our mistakes, messes, and failures, Jesus is still Lord of all. God is always at work in the chaos. His grace is greater than our blunders when we step out and obey his call on our lives.

Another generation is being raised up to "finish the task" in India.

The Messiah has a plan for India, and he will fulfill it before he returns at the Second Coming of Christ:

- Where once there were no Indian missionaries, today there are thousands.
- Where once there were no pastors and elders, today there are millions.
- Where once there were no indigenous church planters, today there are hundreds of thousands.
- Where once there was only a handful of struggling congregations among the untouchable Dalits, there are now tens of thousands.
- Where cruelty, darkness, fear, idolatry, and sin once reigned supreme, there is light and love.
- Where the Word of God was scarcely heard, it is now taught from a thousand points of light.
- Where once Indians were the object of charity, they are now caregivers and disciple makers—sending out aid.
- Where indigenous believers were once seen as parasites on Indian society, they now are contributing to the economy, education, media, and military.

- Where once, the Kingdom of God was seen as an evil invention of alien imperialists, it is now the work of faithful, good men operating multiplication evangelism and discipleship.

And so, the call continues to go out from the Lord of the Harvest! Indians are hearing and answering it—including millions of Hindus and Muslims who are discovering the Jesus Way of living.

"What is God calling you to do?" asks Billy Bray. "It may not be reaching a continent or a nation like India. It may just be raising your family. Running your business. Teaching math. Saving babies or making books. It could be writing computer code!

"It could be starting an NGO, a charity, or a righteous business. Your task is to follow the call of God on your life. That means daily hearing, obeying, believing, uniting and yielding."

"Commit your way unto the Lord, trust also in him; and he will bring it to pass," (Psalm 37:5).

Bibliography

For a complete list of other books in print by Billy Bray, contact the author at bray.william@gmail.com.

If you enjoyed this book, you will also enjoy the following related titles:

Apostolic Adventures by Bob Finley, CA Books
The Calvary Road by Roy Hession, CLC Publications
Revolution in World Missions by K.P. Yohannan
Friend Raising by Betty Barnett, YWAM Publishing
Living in the Light of Eternity by K.P. Yohannan
Messiology by George Verwer, Moody Publishers
Multiply by Frances Chan with Mark Beuving, David C Cook
Pray for the World, 7th edition, by Jason Madryk, IVP Books
Personal Prayer Diary and Daily Planner, by Warren Walsh, YWAM Publishing
Radical by David Platt, Multnomah Books
The Road to Reality by K.P. Yohannan
Warfare Praying by Mark I. Bubeck, Moody Publishers
Why the World Waits by K.P. Yohannan

CPSIA information can be obtained
at www.ICGtesting.com
Printed in the USA
FFOW04n1915280217
32949FF